Contents

Creating Flash Widgets with Flash CS4 and ActionScript 3

by John Arana

If you are a Flash designer or developer and are not making widgets, you're missing out! Creating widgets is a lot of fun and also a great way to make yourself known as a Flash developer. This book shows you how to create Flash widgets with some of the new features introduced in Flash CS4 and ActionScript 3.0. It also shows you how easy it is to make your widgets available on social-networking sites like Facebook and MySpace, while at the same time exploring how to promote and make money off of them. The Internet is being "widgetized," don't miss out on this great opportunity to be a part of it!

For Valena and Isaac

Chapter 1: Introducing Flash Widgets

The presence of Flash on the Internet has been increasing at an astonishing rate since it was released in 1996. It started out as a simple animator and gradually developed into a powerful tool which could be used to create amazing content for the Web. This content came in many forms, including intros, animations, advertisements, games, rich Internet applications, and web sites. Each one of these raised the bar for the presentation layer of the Internet causing a chain reaction in which Flash content ended up on a countless number of web sites. With the onset of social-networking sites, personal home pages, and blogs, a demand for this rich content brought about yet another usage of Flash: *widgets*.

What are Widgets?

Widgets are basically mini-applications that can be embedded into a web page with a snippet of code. This makes widgets both reusable and portable. Some widgets, with slight alterations to the snippet of code, are also user configurable. The term *widget* does not refer to the content but rather to the packaging; in other words, the content of a widget can be virtually anything. Widgets make it possible for people creating or modifying web sites, social profiles, and blogs to include rich content without having to develop it. From tools to games to just plain entertainment, there are thousands of different types of widgets available with new ones being released every day.

Some other names used to describe widgets are gadgets, modules, capsules, minis, snippets, and plug-ins. Different names are used by different sites. For example, they are called *gadgets* on iGoogle, *plug-ins* on WordPress blogs, and *apps* on Facebook and MySpace.

Widgets can be broken down into different types based on the presentation medium. Accordingly, there are desktop widgets, web widgets, and mobile widgets. Although Flash can be used to make all three types, we'll be focusing on web widgets in this book. In addition, Flash is not the only tool used to create widgets, but because most rich content on the Internet is created with Flash, it is definitely at the forefront when it comes to web widgets.

A Brief History of Widgets

The idea of widgets is not a new one. Perhaps the first web widget was the briefly ubiquitous page counter of the nineties. The Java game applet, Trivia Blitz, is another notable web widget from that time. Developed by Uproar.com, this was considered to be the first widget to go "viral," ending up on tens of thousands of web pages. Widgets have come a long way since then, but the general idea is the same: a snippet of code is embedded into a web page, providing the user with a mini-application.

Various types of web sites have contributed to the popularization of widgets on the Internet. Social-networking sites, like Facebook, MySpace, Orkut, and Bebo, have been the most effective in making this happen. Each one of these sites has grown a very large user base and two of them are currently in the global top ten trafficked sites on the Internet (according to the statistics on alexa.com). In addition, the social aspect of these sites makes it easier for widgets to spread fast. Invitations to add the widget, news feeds about it, or simply seeing it on a friends profile page and deciding to add it to your own can lead to a chain reaction where the widget ends up on a countless number of profiles. As a result, social-networking sites are the main contributor to the widespread use of web widgets.

Blogs and their own growing popularity have also greatly contributed to the popularity of widgets. There are many useful widgets for bloggers, including rating systems for posts, sharing components, video players, slideshow creators, and the list goes on. There are also widgets for those interested in blogs. These are sometimes called *Blidgets*, and they basically grab the content from a particular blog and encapsulate it into a portable mini-blog. You can use these to keep track of your favorite blogs without having to visit each one.

Personal home pages, like iGoogle (which is basically a regular Google page with a user-defined set of widgets or "gadgets"), have also played an important part in familiarizing people with the use of widgets. These don't have the social aspect because the person who created it is usually the only one who sees it, but nevertheless they are widely used and a good source of some very cool widgets.

Another important factor to the widespread use of widgets is the various online web sites that provide management and distribution services for widget developers, while at the same time being a good place for users to get widgets. Although there are quite a few sites like this, in this book we'll be focusing on managing and distributing our widget with Widgetbox.com. Using this site, you can easily make your widgets compatible with virtually every social-networking and blogging site.

Widgets have not yet hit their peak in usage or development and there is definitely a lot of room for new ideas and improvements on existing ideas. Your idea, made into a widget, could be the next one to go "viral" and make Internet history.

The Future of Widgets

Widgets are becoming increasingly integrated into various types of web sites. It seems as though the Internet is being "widgetized" and Flash appears to be the tool of choice when it comes to creating these widgets. As more types of widgets are released, the point may come where users can construct an entire web page out of them. Many types of web pages may soon just be an aggregation of assorted widgets. This concept would be similar to the concept of LEGOs, wherein a bunch of widgets could just be "stuck together" to make a web page, blog, or social profile. For example, you would put together a title bar widget, a links widget, a photo slideshow widget, a general content widget, and a guest-book widget, and end up with a robust web page. The content of each would have to be configurable and there would preferably be many choices for each type and each would be customizable in look and feel, preventing all sites that use these widgets from looking the same. This obviously would not take the place of professionally designed web sites, but for social profiles, personal web sites, and blogs it could work well. The Internet may or may not go that far but one thing is for sure, the use and creation of widgets is currently prevalent and expanding every day.

Why Make Flash Widgets?

Other than just for fun, there are many good reasons to create and distribute your own widgets. For one, it's a great way as a developer to get your work out in the open for people to use and give you feedback. Widgets are in demand right now and everything has definitely not been done. A good idea and a bit of design and development could lead to many opportunities as a Flash designer/developer. Also, if you or a client has a web site, a good way to get traffic flowing is the publication of a widget that in some way represents or relates to the site, while still being useful or entertaining. Finally, if that is not enough, you can also make money off of your widgets, which will be discussed later in this book.

Summary

In this chapter, widgets were defined and their history was briefly discussed. Some ideas into the future of widgets and a couple of good reasons to start developing your own Flash widgets were also presented. In the next chapter, you'll be looking at the new features in Flash CS4 and upgrading to ActionScript 3.0, if you haven't already.

Chapter 2: Migrating to Flash CS4 and ActionScript 3.0

Over the years Flash has been transformed from a basic animation tool into a full-featured IDE (Integrated Development Environment) with the tools and components to tackle virtually any development. ActionScript has also evolved since its introduction with Flash as a simple scripting language with a very limited set of actions. Now it's a robust, object-oriented programming language, which can be used to build complex games, applications, and web sites. In this chapter, I'll discuss some of the key additions and improvements included in Flash CS4 and I'll try to get you stubborn AS2'ers (I used to be one too) upgraded to ActionScript 3.0.

What's New and Different in Flash CS4

The changes in Flash CS4 are definitely something to be excited about. Overall, the look and feel is better and the default layout is, in my opinion, more intuitive but still user configurable. There are many new tools and features that make it easy to do complex operations that previously required quite a bit of ActionScript. This includes some basic 3D manipulation of objects, a very cool inverse kinematics tool, and an intricate motion editor to refine your animations.

Using the New Tools

There are quite a few new tools being introduced in Flash CS4 and they are all very handy. Since this isn't a full primer on the subject, I will only be going over the tools used in the widget example (don't worry they happen to be the coolest ones). The two new tools I'll be discussing are the 3D Rotation Tool and the Bone Tool. They are fairly complex and have quite a few configurations to learn about. Remember, I'll be using these tools in the example widget so follow along.

The 3D Rotation Tool

The 3D Rotation Tool resides in the tool bar, below the Free Transform Tool and above the Lasso Tool. It provides graphical controls around the object being manipulated and input configurations within the Properties Window when it is active. In the following example, you'll be taking text and making some 3D changes to it, while at the same time creating a tween.

1. Open Flash CS4 then open a new file by selecting File ➤ New ➤ Flash File (ActionScript 3.0).

2. Select the Text Tool (T) and type your name (or whatever you want) on the stage, in any font, and make it a fairly large size.

3. Using the Selection Tool (V), select your text, select Modify ➤ Convert to Symbol (F8), and convert it to a movie clip with the name *text*.

4. Now select the 3D Transformation Tool (W). If your movie clip was still selected, you should see two concentric circles and a crosshair in front of your movie clip as shown in Figure 2-1.

Figure 2-1. The graphical interface to the 3D Transformation Tool. Also, notice in the Properties tab, under the Position and Size heading, there is a new 3D Position and View section with a new set of properties listed.

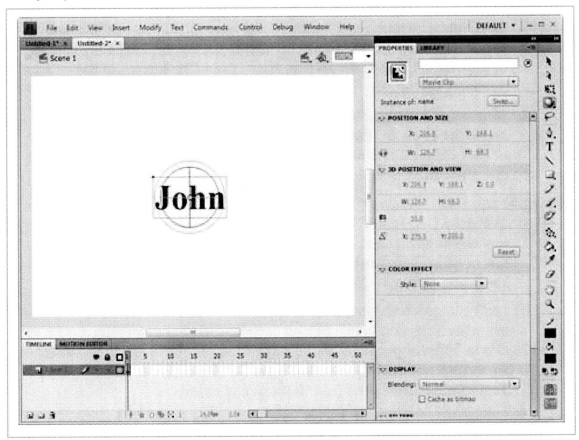

5. In the timeline, click the 10th frame and select Insert ➤ Timeline ➤ Frame (F5) to insert frames up to that point. Click one of these newly created frames and select Insert ➤ Motion Tween.

6. Next, make sure your selected frame is 10 and move your mouse up to your movie clip. Hover your mouse above the green horizontal line and notice the small "y" that shows up next to the cursor. This indicates the axis which that access point controls. Click down on it then drag it up and down. Notice that as you drag it, one of the sectors fills in to a

certain degree, indicating how much the object has changed position on the y axis. Move it about 45 degrees in any direction and let go. Look down at the timeline and notice a keyframe has already been created for you (any change in position will automatically do this).

7. Click frame 20 and insert frames, hover over the red vertical line and notice the small "x" that shows up next to the cursor, indicating control of the x axis. Click down on it, move it about 120 degrees in any direction, and let go.

8. Now insert frames up to frame 30, hover over the inner blue circle and notice the small "z" that shows up next to the cursor, indicating control of the z axis. Click down on it, move it about 180 degrees in any direction, and let go.

9. Next, insert frames up to frame 40, then click on the outer orange circle and move your mouse all around. Notice that this is controlling movement on all axes. Leave it in any position you'd like (preferably one in which you can read the text) and you should now have 5 keyframes across 40 frames on the timeline.

10. Lastly, to give your animation a little more movement on the stage, using the Selection Tool, click on each keyframe and drag the movie clip to different positions on the stage. You now have created a tween. An example of this is shown in Figure 2-2. To watch it, select Control ➤ Test Movie (Ctrl+Enter/Cmd+Return) and enjoy.

Note   If the rotation of the movie clip on the x, y, and z axes does not make sense to you, the following should clear it up. For the x axis, imagine a horizontal pole going through the center of your movie clip, from left to right, and picture how it would spin on it. Now, for the y axis, imagine a vertical pole going through the center of your movie clip, from top to bottom, and picture its movement around it. For the z axis, imagine a pole going from the front of your movie clip to the back of it, right through the center, and see how it would rotate on it.

Figure 2-2. The lines indicate the motion of the object from keyframe to keyframe, while the small dots across the lines show the number of frames between each keyframe.

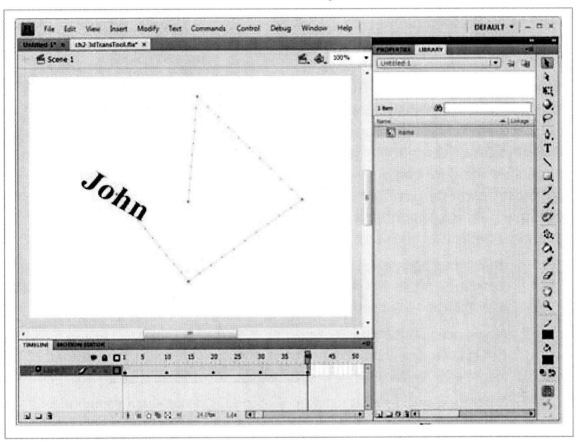

TIP   You can also adjust and curve your tweens by simply clicking and dragging the red lines that indicate the path of motion. That's right, no more need for motion guide layers!

There is definitely much more you could do to improve this example, like making the animation more of a seamless loop, adding a filter effects, or adjusting the easing for more interesting motions, but there is a lot to discuss, so let's move on.

The Bone Tool

This tool is truly awesome! It gives you the power to connect objects (with "bones") and it automatically creates a motion relationship between the objects for you. This relationship, known as IK (Inverse Kinematics), describes how the motion of something affects, or is limited by, the motion of another thing to which it's connected. Each bone can be configured to have a different range of motion, defined by degrees. In the following example, you'll be creating a simple arm out of circles and create an animation with its movement.

1. Start by opening a new Flash file and selecting the Oval Tool (O). Draw a circle on the stage (about 100 pixels wide), select it, and convert it into a movie clip with the name circle.

2. Now open your Library by selecting Window ➤ Library (Ctrl+L/Cmd+L) and drag two more instances of your circle onto the stage. You should now have three circles in view.

3. Select one and shrink it to about 80 pixels wide and high using the Free Transform Tool (Q) or by entering the values in the Properties Window. Do the same thing to one of the other circles, but this time shrink it to 60 pixels.

4. Next, put the three circles next to each other, largest to smallest, from left to right, as shown in Figure 2-3.

Figure 2-3. The three circles in position, which will act as portions of an arm.

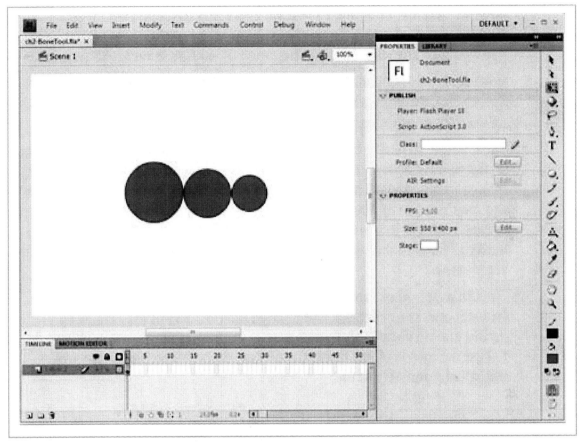

5. Select the Bone Tool (X) and click in the center of the large circle drag to the middle of the medium circle and let go. Notice this makes a visual connection between the two circles.

6. Now do the same thing from the medium circle to the small circle. Notice the circle outlines around the joints (in the large and medium circles). These indicate the range of movement in each particular joint, which is currently 360 degrees–no constraint.

7. Click on the "bone" between the large and medium circles and notice the configurations available in the Properties Window. Under the Joint: Rotation section, click the Constrain checkbox and enter –90 degrees for the Min and 90 degrees for the Max. Notice the outline around the joint is now a half circle, indicating the range of motion is now 180 degrees.

8. Now click on the "bone" between the medium and small circles and again, click the Constrain checkbox in the Joint: Rotation section. Then set the Min to –60 degrees and the Max to 60 degrees.

9. Click frame 10 and select Insert ➤ Timeline ➤ Frame (F5) to add frames to that point. Click and drag the small circle around and observe how its change in position affects the medium circle. Also, notice how the large and medium constrains limit the motions of the medium and small circles. Leave it in a position that is different from the one in which it started. This will automatically create a keyframe on frame 10, resulting in a tween.

10. To add some more movement, click through frames 20, 30, and 40 and for each one, insert frames and change the position of the arm. You should end up with 5 keyframes across 40 frames as shown in Figure 2-4. Test the movie (Ctrl+Enter/Cmd+Return) and watch how the arm realistically moves around.

Note You can also set your Bone Tool creations up for runtime manipulation (by the user). To do this, all you have to do is set the Type under the Options section in the Properties menu to *Runtime* instead of *Authortime*. You can't have any preset animation if you choose this option.

Figure 2-4. The 3 circles connected using the Bone Tool, set in different positions across 40 frames to create an animation.

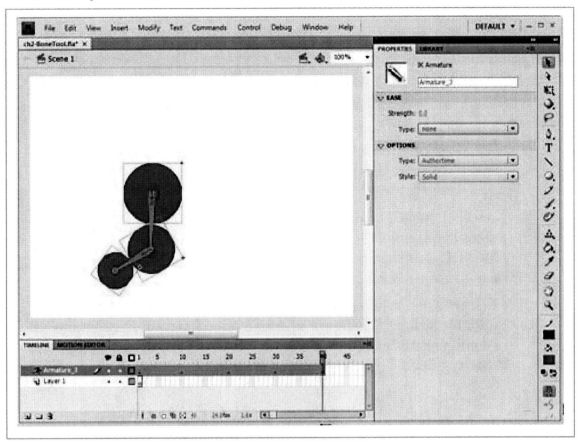

The Bone Tool is definitely a powerful addition to the Flash toolset. You could create the same effects with ActionScript, which is necessary when you want the motion to be dynamic, but for simple, planned animations, this tool is perfect.

Introducing the Motion Editor

The Motion Editor is a nice addition and is basically a zoom-in to the Timeline on a particular tween. It lets you add keyframes and make changes to multiple aspects of the object over time. These aspects include filter, color, skew, scale, rotation, and ease of the object being tweened. The following example will go over basic usage of the Motion Editor interface.

1. Start by opening a new Flash file and selecting the Rectangle Tool (R). Draw a square on the left side of the stage (about 100 pixels wide), select it, and convert it into a movie clip with the name *square*.

2. Now click frame 20 and select Insert ➤ Timeline ➤ Frame (F5) to add frames to that point. With the 20th frame still selected, click Insert ➤ Motion Tween, then move the square to the right side of the stage (automatically creating a keyframe).

3. Click anywhere within the tween in the Timeline and open the Motion Editor by clicking Window ➤ Motion Editor. Notice it is a complex grid of configurations as shown in Figure 2-5, with the columns being: Property, Value, Ease, Keyframe, and Graph.

Figure 2-5. The Motion Editor. Under the Basic Motion section, "X" is a graph which starts low and goes high (indicating the change in position you made over 20 frames).

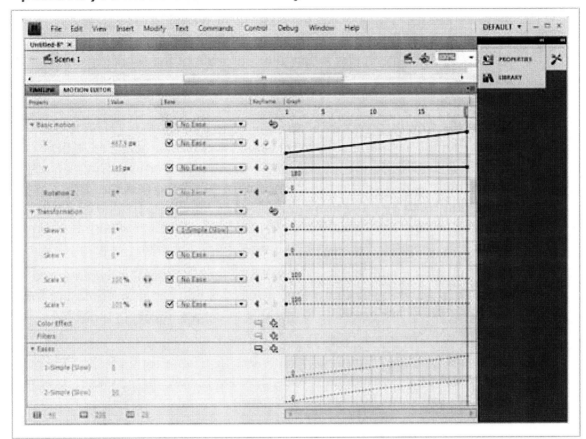

4. Look at the bottom left of the window. There are three symbols with numbers next to them. The first two are configurations for the height of each row (the second one for rows in a selected, expanded state). The third one is for configuring how many frames are visible in the graph. Change this one to 20, so you can see the full length of your tween without having to scroll.

5. The graph works like the timeline in that you can add keyframes. Once you have at least two keyframes, you can click and drag them up or down to create a change in a particular property throughout the in-between frames. You can use the controls provided in the Keyframe column to move from one keyframe to another and alter the values by just typing them in. So, let's first alter the scale of the square by adding a keyframe on frame 20 of the Scale X and Scale Y rows (in the Transformation section).

6. Now make sure their properties are linked to one another. (Next to the values there is a chain that is either linked together or detached. Click this if it is detached to link the X and Y scaling properties.) Click on one of the newly added keyframes to ensure the playhead is at the 20th frame (indicated by a red vertical line). Now change the value of Scale X to 200 percent and Scale Y should automatically change with it. From frame 1 to frame 20, the square will now double in size.

7. Next, look down and find the Filters section, press the plus symbol, and select Drop Shadow. Notice all the properties you can now configure for this filter. Some are graphed, being able to change throughout the timeline, and some are static.

8. Let's start with the Blur properties. Add a keyframe for both Blur X and Blur Y at frame 20. Now make sure they are linked, the playhead is over frame 20, and enter in a value of 15 pixels.

9. Move your playhead over frame 1 and change the Strength property to 75 percent, the Quality property to "High," the Angle property to 90 degrees, and the Distance property to 1 pixel.

10. Add keyframes to the 20th frame of the Strength and Distance properties and change Strength to 25 percent and Distance to 20 pixels.

11. Go back to the Timeline, select your tween, and click Edit ➤ Timeline ➤ Copy Frames to copy it. Then paste it by selecting the 21st frame and clicking Edit ➤ Timeline ➤ Paste Frames. Now click the newly pasted tween, right-click (Ctrl+click) and select Reverse Keyframes to reverse the animation.

12. Select Control ➤ Test Movie (Ctrl+Enter/Cmd+Return) to see what you've made.

Definitely not the coolest animation, but it is still somewhat complex because of all the property changes it goes through. Feel free to explore all the different configurations you can make with the Motion Editor before moving on. It is a good tool to know if you do most your animations within the Flash IDE.

Now that you're familiar with the some of the new Flash CS4 tools, I'm going to leave the Flash IDE and discuss ActionScript 3.0. If you're already familiar with ActionScript 3.0, you may skip ahead to the next chapter.

Moving Up to ActionScript 3.0

ActionScript 3.0 (AS3) was released with Flash CS3 and the changes were so fundamental that not everyone has come up to speed. Making the upgrade is inevitable (resistance is futile) and you won't regret it. There is a lot more you can do in this version and the way things generally work makes more sense and aligns with the standards, making your programming skills more transferable with other languages. It would be beyond the scope of this book to give a full dissertation on the changes in AS3, but I will discuss some basics, especially the AS3 relevant to the example widget you'll be developing. Other than that, I'll direct you to some good sources on the subject, so you can find out everything you'll need to know about AS3.

AS3 is completely class based and the structure of classes is a bit different. Classes are now held in a package syntax which you can import other packages to for usage in your class.

```
package {
    import flash.events.MouseEvent;
    import flash.display.MovieClip;
    public class MyClass {
    }
}
```

You can also assign your own package structure based on the folder organization of your classes, as shown in Figure 2-6 and the following snippet of code:

```
package com.yourdomain.utils {
    public class Utility {
    }
}
```

Figure 2-6. The folder structure necessary for the above example.

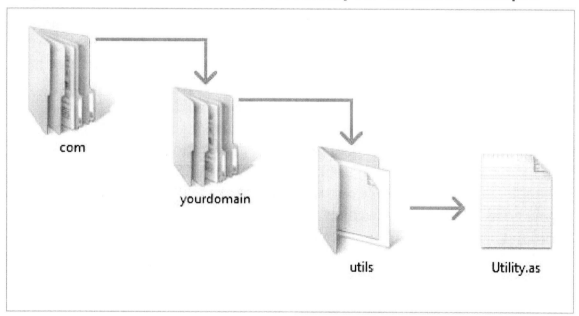

In Flash CS3 and CS4 you can now assign a class, called the "Document Class," to a Flash file which automatically gets called upon running the movie. To assign a document class, enter in the name of your class in the Class field of the Properties Window, as shown in Figure 2-7. This class must extend the MovieClip or Sprite class, like in the following:

```
package {
    import flash.display.MovieClip;
    public class MyClass extends MovieClip {
        public function MyClass() {
        }
    }
}
```

Figure 2-7. The Class field of the Properties Window where you can designate your document class.

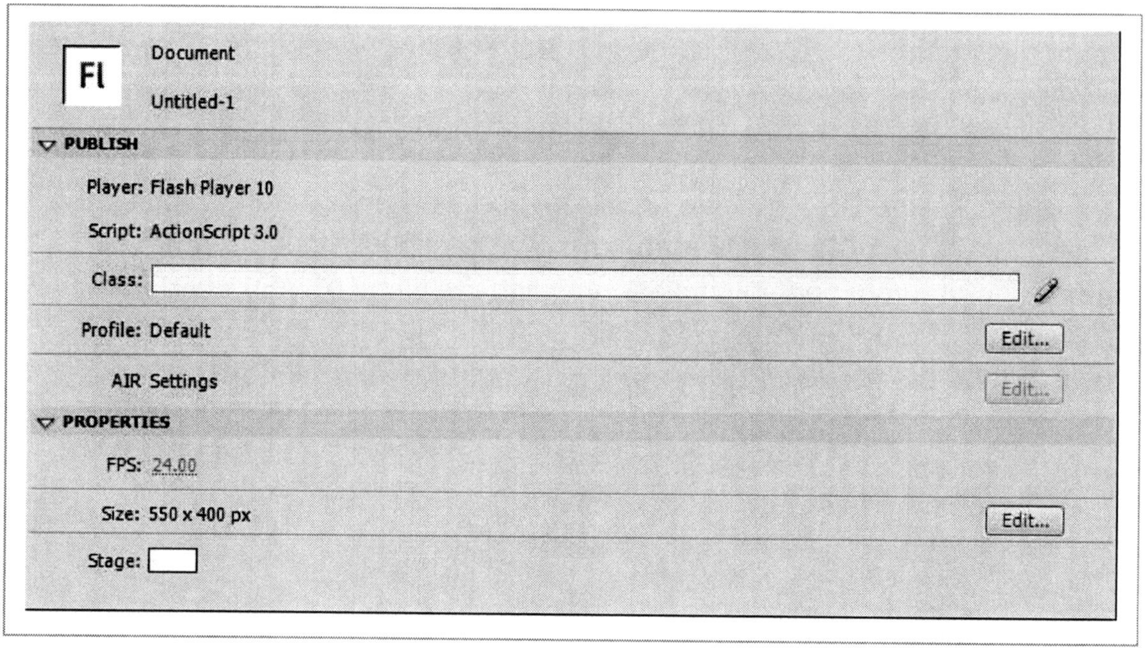

Note　　The Sprite class is new to ActionScript 3.0 and is basically the functionality of a movie clip without the timeline. You can only extend Sprite as a Document class when there is no ActionScript within the Timeline of your Flash movie.

There are also many little syntax changes in AS3, which at first can be a little annoying, but they end up making sense.

The properties of display objects have been renamed and the underscores removed, as shown in the following list:

AS3	AS2
mc.x	mc._x
mc.y	mc._y
mc.width	mc._width
mc.height	mc._height
mc.rotation	mc._rotation
mc.mouseX	mc._xmouse
mc.mouseY	mc._ymouse
mc.parent	mc._parent

In AS2, when a function did not return anything you used:

```
function myFunction( ):Void{
```

In AS3, it is the same except in lowercase form:

```
function myFunction( ):void {
```

Tip   When converting your AS2 code to AS3, you can speed up the process by using Find and Replace (Ctrl+F/Cmd+F) to replace code like "Void" with "void" and "_x" with "x".

In AS2, values that represented percent were expressed as 0–100, like in the following:

```
mc._alpha = 30;
```

In AS3, they are now expressed in the 0–1 range. For example, 30 percent would be represented like this:

```
mc.alpha = 0.3;
```

The drawing API is now accessed through the new `graphics` object which is included in the `MovieClip` and `Sprite` classes.

For example, in AS2:

```
mc.lineStyle(1,0x0000FF);
mc.lineTo(0,100);
```

and in AS3:

```
mc.graphics.lineStyle(1,0x0000FF);
mc.graphics.lineTo(0,100);
```

Also, there are now new graphics functions to draw shapes, like in the following:

```
mc.graphics.drawRect(0,0,100,100);
```

This draws a rectangle at 0 x and 0 y (the first and second arguments), with 100 pixels width and 100 pixels height (the third and fourth arguments).

Another change is how missing arguments to a function are handled. In AS2 the arguments passed to a function were all optional and defaulted to null. In AS3, all arguments are required unless a default value is given, as in the following example:

```
function drawCircle(radius:Number, ➥
color:Number=0x000000){
}
drawCircle();//results in an error
drawCircle(3);//works because color defaults to black
```

Another nice change is that in AS2 when you listened to the roll over of a button, the function that handled this would be out of the scope of the class and in the scope of the button. You could remedy this with the `Delegate` class but now it automatically stays within the scope of the class.

```
//AS2
myButton.onRollOver = handleRollOver;
myButton.onRollOut = Delegate.create(this, ↪
handleRollOut);
function handleRollOver() {
    //in the scope of the buton
}
function handleRollOut() {
    //in the scope of the class
}

//AS3
myButton.addEventListener(MouseEvent.ROLL_OVER, ↪
handleRollOver);
function handleRollOver(evt:MouseEvent) {
    //in the scope of the class
}
```

Notice in the AS3 example, the roll over event is listened to differently than it is in the AS2 example. AS3 provides this single way of handling events which is more clear-cut and standard than the multiple ways provided in AS2. The parameters sent to addEventListener are the name of the event you're listening to and the function that should be called when the event is fired. The name of the event is just a string, in this case "rollOver," but it is good practice to use the constants available within the built-in event classes. The following would still work though:

```
myButton.addEventListener("rollOver", handleRollOver);
```

An event is fired when dispatchEvent is called:

```
dispatchEvent(new MouseEvent(MouseEvent.ROLL_OVER));
```

You can also dispatch custom events:

```
addEventListener("itIsDone", handleItIsDone);
dispatchEvent(new Event("itIsDone"));
```

Also, notice in the signature of the AS3 `handleRollOver` method a parameter is expected. Every event handler is automatically passed an event object which gives info about the event and reference to the target of the event.

Another major change to the language is how movie clips are added and removed to the stage and to other movie clips. In AS2, `createEmptyMovieClip`, `attachMovieClip`, and `removeMovieClip` were used. In AS3, instantiation of a display object and `addChild` or `removeChild` is used, as shown in the following:

```
var mc = new MovieClip();
mc.drawRectangle(0,0,100,100);
addChild(mc);
```

There is also a difference in how data is sent and loaded from external sources. There is no more `LoadVars` or `loadVariables`. In AS3, there is a new set of classes that handle this, `URLLoader`, `URLRequest`, and `URLVariables`. The `URLLoader` class is used to download data from a URL as text, binary data, or URL-encoded variables. The `URLRequest` class holds the URL and other information for the about the HTTP request. The `URLVariables` class holds any variables you wish to send with your request. The following example shows how all three of these are used to send variables to a PHP file.

```
var url:String = "test.php";
var request:URLRequest = new URLRequest(url);
request.method = URLRequestMethod.POST;
var variables:URLVariables = new URLVariables();
variables.varA = "Bob";
variables.varB = "1234";
request.data = variables;
var loader = new URLLoader();
loader.load(request);
```

You can also use these classes to load text and xml files, as you will see with our widget example.

Although we don't use it in this book, there is also a separate class, Loader, used to load SWF and image files. Here is an example of how to use it:

```
var loader = new Loader();
loader.contentLoaderInfo.addEventListener(↵
Event.COMPLETE,onLoaded);
loader.load(new URLRequest("myPic.jpg"));
addChild(loader);
function onLoaded (evt:Event):void {
    //myPic.jpg is now loaded
}
```

In AS3, there is also a new model for sound playback. The Sound class represents a sound that can be played and SoundChannel holds and can control a sound that is playing.

```
sound = new Sound();
channel = sound.play();
```

In this example, you could also add an event to SoundChannel that fires when sound has finished playing or use it to check the position of sound while it is playing.

The last change we'll be going over is the addition of the Timer class. The AS2 way of handling time based actions, setInterval and clearInterval, are still available in AS3 but the new Timer class follows the AS3 event model and is overall a better way to handle time based events. Here is how it works:

```
var seconds:Number = 0;
var timer:Timer = new Timer(1000,5);
timer.addEventListener(TimerEvent.TIMER,onTimer);
myTimer.start();
function onTimer(evt:TimerEvent):void {
    seconds++;
    trace(seconds);
}
```

Remember, for every class there is a package you must import. The following is a list of the classes we went over and their package names:

CLASS	PACKAGE
MouseEvent	flash.events
MovieClip	flash.display
Sprite	flash.display
Loader	flash.display
URLLoader	flash.net
URLRequest	flash.net
URLVariables	flash.net
URLRequestMethod	flash.net
Sound	flash.media
SoundChannel	flash.media
Timer	flash.utils

Notice many of these classes share the same package. Although it is not always considered good practice, you can import all classes that you use from a package by using the wildcard symbol as in the following:

```
Import flash.display.*;
import flash.net.*;
import flash.media.*;
```

There are many more important changes and additions to AS3 which I encourage you to explore, but this book is short and we must move on. Here are some resources to help you find out more about AS3:

First, for a general language migration list, go to `http://livedocs.adobe.com/flex/2/langref/migration.html` and print it out, then tape it on your wall (at least that's what I did, and it definitely helped things go a bit smoother). Don't just read through the whole thing. Instead, use it as a reference or you may get overwhelmed with all the changes.

Next, to get an in-depth tutorial on the subject, check out `http://www.senocular.com/flash/tutorials/as3withflashcs3/` and bookmark it for future reference. This tutorial covers a brief history of ActionScript, basic differences in the new version, object-oriented programming, and various other helpful topics.

Then, for a good book on the subject, get *Foundation ActionScript 3.0 with Flash CS3 and Flex* by Sean McSharry, Steve Webster, and Todd Yard (friends of ED, 2007). This book will teach you all the fundamentals and then some. You can buy it as an eBook on `www.friendsofed.com` or, if you're not down with virtual books, you can get a hard copy at Amazon.

Last, visit and bookmark `http://livedocs.adobe.com/flash/9.0/ActionScriptLangRefV3/` for a list and description of all the AS3 classes.

Summary

In this chapter, you learned how to use a couple of the new tools introduced in Flash CS4. You also took a good look at the new Motion Editor and explored some of the language changes in AS3. In the next chapter, you will use these new tools and AS3 to create your widget.

Chapter 3: Developing Your First Widget

The first step to any development is the defining of an idea. Although this sounds obvious, it is a task that doesn't always get completed because it is easy to get excited and start development too soon. This results in a slow, rigid process because your specifications are not in place to guide you. To avoid this, I will discuss how to thoroughly complete this first step of defining an idea then how to further define your abstract idea in enough detail so that it can be expressed in reality. Finally, I'll make a step-by-step list to organize the production and guide you smoothly through development. This list will comprise the steps included in the design of the interface (what the user sees and interacts with) and the writing of the ActionScript, which is the logic behind the scenes.

Creating the Idea

Fortunately, when trying to think of an idea for a Flash widget, you're not very limited. Imagine anything and you could probably make it into a widget. The most successful widgets aren't of a certain type. In fact, if you look at the top three widgets on WidgetBox.com, you'll see that they're all different. Currently, there is a nostalgic game, a pregnancy counter, and a virtual pet widget in the top three spots. Each one is a completely different type of widget. The game is entertainment, the pregnancy counter is a useful tool, and the virtual pet is just a cute addition to your page. Complexity is also not a determining factor when it comes to the success of your widget. As long as people like it, even if it's just a rock with a happy face on it, your widget has the potential to become popular. People like simplicity and sometimes silly ideas you come up with on a whim will go a lot further than you would think.

It is true that many of the ideas you'll think of have already been developed into widgets. Don't let this stop you! There is always room for alterations in look and feel as well as improvements in functionality and user experience. Without improvements on existing ideas, there would be no evolution of music, art, or science. Just make sure you add some of your own ideas!

If you're having trouble thinking of a widget to make, there are some exercises you can do to help spark an idea. One way is to look at all the categories for widgets: Education, Family, Finance, Games, Politics, News, Humor, Movies, and many more. Now think of the activities people do in each of these categories—that should get ideas flowing a bit. For example, you could come up with an entertaining idea like a joke of the day widget for the Humor category or a useful idea like a mortgage calculator for the Finance category. Then you can spice up these general ideas with original ways to represent them, like a slot-machine mortgage calculator or floating bubbles that display the first part of a joke which the user pops to see the punch line. Another way to think of some widget ideas is to just look at real things people use or have and find ways to represent them in the virtual world. In this case, you could make an old-school boom box that plays various loops embedded into it. You could also make a pet fish that swims around in a fish bowl, which users can feed and watch get bigger and bigger. Sometimes ideas for widgets will just pop out of the blue and be great, but for the times when you just can't think of anything, the few exercises I've covered can help jumpstart your creativity.

For your widget example you will be making a dancing robot. This may not be the best idea for a widget, but it is one that will allow you to use the tools you learned about in the previous chapter and it will work well with the features you'll be adding in the next chapter. The example will also work well for those of you who would like to stay creative while learning how to do this, because you can draw your robot in any style. So, before you start making this, let's define it in greater detail.

Here is a list of the graphics you'll need for your robot:

- A head, including any facial features
- A neck
- A torso
- Arms, which will be split up to enable the Inverse Kinematics (IK)
- Legs, which will also be split up for IK

Additionally, we'll need to create:

- Keyframes, which show the robot in different dance positions
- A basic room for the robot to dance in
- A message board, which will display a message at the top of the screen
- ActionScript to control the robot

With those aspects figured out, you can now easily create your step-by-step development list:

1. Create robot head, neck, torso, arms, and legs.
2. Use the Bone Tool to attach parts of the robot body.
3. Keyframe the robot in different positions.
4. Draw the room and message board.
5. Import the music.
6. Write ActionScript to control the robot.

Designing the Graphics

Now that you have your steps figured out, you can go ahead with development. First you will be creating the graphics and then you will write the ActionScript. I am going to keep the robot graphically very simple so as not to stray too far from the purpose of this book. Remember, feel free to draw your robot in any style you would like, but make sure you follow the steps for creating and naming the movie clips out of each part. These are needed for the Inverse Kinematics and ActionScript you'll be doing later. Also, if you don't want to draw the robot, you can download this example at www.CreateFlashWidgets.com/book/robot.zip.

Creating the Robot

1. Start by opening a new Flash file and saving it as *robot.fla* (we'll be using the default stage size of 550 x 400).

2. Select the Oval Tool (O) and draw a light gray oval about 100 x 50 pixels, select it, and convert it to a movie clip with the name *head*. Give this movie clip an instance name of *head* in the Properties Window so you can access it with ActionScript. Now select it and click Edit ➤ Edit Symbols (Ctrl+E/Cmd+E) so you can add some facial features.

3. Use the Oval Tool to draw a blue circle about 20 x 20 pixels, select it, and convert it to a movie clip with the name *eye*. Next drag another instance of it to the stage from the library and position the eyes. Then give the left eye an instance name of *leftEye* and the right eye an instance name of *rightEye*.

4. While you're still in the *head* timeline, select the Rectangle Tool (R) and draw a dark gray rectangle about 25 x 5 pixels, convert it to a movie clip with the name *mouth*, and place it below the eyes.

5. Select the two eyes and the mouth and add a Drop Shadow filter by clicking the small Add Filter icon on the bottom left of the Filters section (found in the Properties Window). Configure it by setting Blur X and Blur Y to 3 pixels, Strength to 50 percent, Quality to High, Distance to 3 pixels, and by checking the Inner Shadow checkbox. Figure 3-1 shows the completed head.

Figure 3-1. The head and face of the robot.

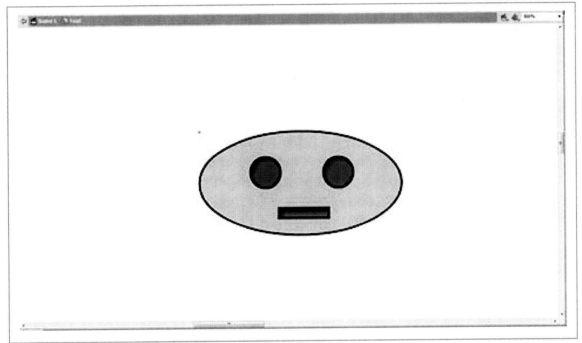

6. Now return to the main timeline by selecting Edit ➤ Edit Document (Ctrl+E/Cmd+E). Use the Rectangle Tool to draw a light gray rectangle about 10 x 20 pixels and convert it to a movie clip with the name *neck*.

7. Next draw a light gray rectangle with the Rectangle Tool about 90 x 100 pixels and turn it into a movie clip with the name *torso*.

8. Click the neck and select Modify ➤ Arrange ➤ Send to Back (Alt+Shift+Down/Option+Shift+Down) to place the neck behind the torso and head. Now position the neck and torso below the head, while keeping about a third of the neck under the head and a third under the torso (you do this to prevent the edges from being exposed when it's moving).

9. Select the Oval Tool and draw a light gray circle about 32 x 32 pixels and convert it to a movie clip with the name *shoulder*.

10. Next select the Rectangle Tool and draw a light gray rectangle about 60 x 18 pixels and convert it to a movie clip with the name *upperArm*.

11. For the lower arm, it will be a combination of three parts: the elbow, the forearm, and the hand. Start with the elbow by selecting the Oval Tool and draw a 25 x 25 pixel, light gray circle and convert it to a movie clip with the name *elbow*. Now for the forearm, select the Rectangle Tool to draw a 40 x 15 pixel, light gray rectangle and convert it to a movie clip with the name *forearm*. For the hand, draw three small rectangles, about 24 x 10 pixels each, place them in a "c" formation, and convert them to a movie clip named *hand*.

12. Now place the forearm so the edge of it is to about the middle of the elbow, select Modify ➤ Arrange ➤ Send to Back to place it under the elbow. Attach the hand, select all three parts, and turn them into a movie clip with the name *lowerArm*.

13. Position the shoulder over the top-right edge of the torso and attach the upper arm, overlapping the shoulder at about the center of it. With the upper arm still selected, select Modify ➤ Arrange ➤ Send to Back to place it behind the shoulder.

14. Next attach the lower arm to the upper arm, overlapping it to about the middle of the elbow. Figure 3-2 shows the completed arm.

Figure 3-2. The arm of the robot.

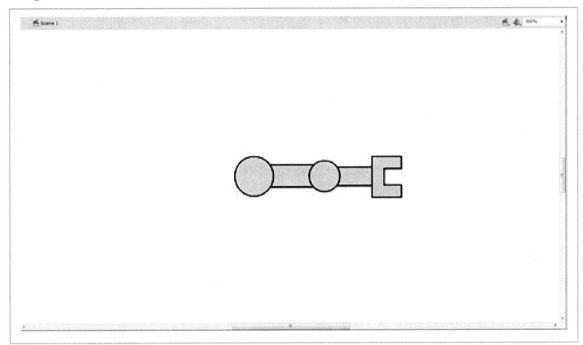

15. Select the shoulder, upper arm, and lower arm. Then copy the clips (Edit ➤ Copy or Ctrl+C/Cmd+C), paste them onto the canvas (Edit ➤ Paste or Ctrl+C/Cmd+V), and mirror it (Modify ➤ Transform ➤ Flip Horizontal). Now move it over to the top-left side of the torso.

16. The leg is similar in construction to the arm. First you create the hip by selecting the Oval Tool and drawing a light gray circle about 36 x 36 pixels and convert it to a movie clip with the name *hip*.

17. Next select the Rectangle Tool and draw a light gray rectangle about 25 x 60 pixels and convert it to a movie clip with the name *upperLeg*.

18. The lower leg, like the lower arm, will be a combination of three parts: the knee, the shin, and the foot. Start with the knee by selecting the Oval Tool and draw a 30 x 30 pixel, light gray circle and convert it to a movie clip with the name *knee*.

19. Now for the shin, select the Rectangle Tool and draw a 20 x 50 pixel, light gray rectangle and convert it to a movie clip with the name *shin*. For the foot, draw a rectangle about 44 x 18 pixels and convert it to a movie clip with the name *foot*.

20. Now place the shin so the top of it touches the middle of the knee, select Modify ➤ Arrange ➤ Send to Back to place it under the knee. Attach the foot, select all three parts, and convert them to a movie clip with the name *lowerLeg*.

21. Position the hip over the bottom-right edge of the torso and attach the upper leg, overlapping the hip's center. With the upper leg still selected, select Modify ➤ Arrange ➤ Send to Back to place it behind the hip.

22. Next attach the lower leg to the upper leg, overlapping it at about the middle of the knee. Figure 3-3 shows the completed leg.

Figure 3-3. The leg of the robot.

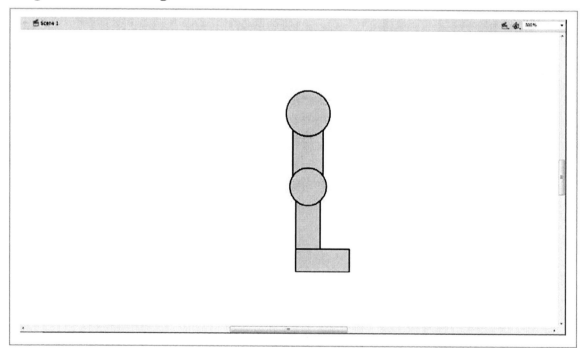

23. Select the hip, upper leg, and lower leg. Then copy the clips (Edit ➤ Copy or Ctrl+C/Cmd+C), paste them onto the canvas (Edit ➤ Paste or Ctrl+V/Cmd+V), and mirror it (Modify ➤ Transform ➤ Flip Horizontal). Now move it over to the bottom-left side of the torso.

24. Select the whole robot and add a Bevel filter by clicking the small Add Filter icon on the bottom left of the Filters section (found in the Properties Window). Set Blur X and Blur Y to 3 pixels, Strength to 50 percent, Quality to High, and Distance to 5 pixels.

25. With the whole robot still selected, convert it to a movie clip with the name *robot*. Then give this movie clip an instance name of *robot* in the Properties Window.

26. Save your progress (Ctrl+S/Cmd+S).

You should now have a full robot to work with as shown in Figure 3-4. Next you will be attaching parts of the robot with the Bone Tool and configuring the rotational constraints, making it easier for us to position it in different dance moves.

Figure 3-4. The robot with all its parts drawn and positioned.

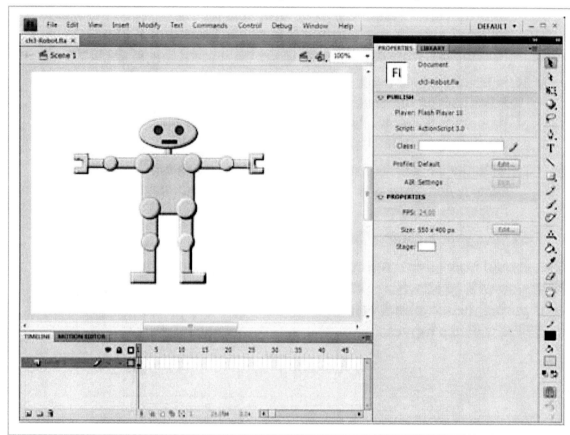

Connecting the Robot

1. Start by selecting the robot movie clip and clicking Edit ➤ Edit Symbol (Ctrl+E/Cmd+E) to enter its timeline.

2. Select the Bone Tool (X), click and drag from the center of the right shoulder to the center of the upper arm. Next click and drag from the center of the upper arm to the center of the elbow. Now do the same step with the other arm.

3. With the Bone Tool still selected, click and drag from the center of the right hip to the center of the upper leg. Next click and drag from the

center of the upper leg to the center of the knee. Now do the same step with the other leg.

4. With the Bone Tool still selected, click and drag from the center of the neck to the center of the head.

Note   When connecting movie clips with the Bone Tool, layers in the Timeline are created and the movie clips involved in the connection are moved to the new layer. This can create unwanted depth changes with your movie clips (like the torso being behind the neck). This can be fixed by moving the layers up or down in the Timeline. Also, using the Bone Tool can change the depths of your movie clips within the same layer. When you are finished creating the bones, fix the depths of the parts if they are incorrect by using Modify ➤ Arrange ➤ Send Backward or Send to Back and Modify ➤ Arrange ➤ Send Forward or Send to Front.

You are done creating the bones but now you must constrain their motion.

5.   First click the bone that connects the right shoulder to the right upper arm. Under the Joint: Rotation section in the Properties Window, click the Constrain checkbox and enter –70 degrees for the Min and 110 degrees for the Max.

6.   Now click the bone that connects the left shoulder to the left upper arm, click the Joint: Rotation Constrain check box, and enter –110 degrees for the Min and 70 degrees for the Max.

7.   Next click the bone that connects the right upper arm to the right lower arm, click the Joint: Rotation Constrain checkbox, and enter –5 degrees for the Min and 5 degrees for the Max.

8.   Click the bone that connects the left upper arm to the right lower arm, click the Joint: Rotation Constrain checkbox, and enter –5 degrees for the Min and 5 degrees for the Max.

That's it for the arms, now to the legs.

9. Click the bone that connects the right hip to the right upper leg, select the Joint: Rotation Constrain checkbox, and enter −110 degrees for the Min and 45 degrees for the Max.

10. Now click the bone that connects the left hip to the left upper leg, select the Joint: Rotation Constrain checkbox, and enter −45 degrees for the Min and 110 degrees for the Max.

11. Next click the bone that connects the right upper leg to the right lower leg, select the Joint: Rotation Constrain checkbox, and enter 5 degrees for the Min and 5 degrees for the Max.

12. Then click the bone that connects the left upper leg to the left lower leg, select the Joint: Rotation Constrain checkbox, and enter −5 degrees for the Min and 5 degrees for the Max.

13. Click the bone that connects the neck to the head, select the Joint:Rotation Constrain checkbox, and enter −25 degrees for the Min and 25 degrees for the Max.

14. Save your progress (Ctrl+S/Cmd+S).

Tip   It's a good idea to go through each layer that was created by the Bone Tool and name it according to the part of the robot. This will help in the next step by making it easier to keep track of which parts you have moved and which you haven't for each frame.

Once these steps are complete, feel free to use the selection tool to move the arms, legs, and head around to see how the Inverse Kinematics works on each. Now that you have your robot ready to go, let's set up the different dance positions.

Keyframing the Dance Moves

The next step is easy and fun. You will just need to add frames and move the robot around in different positions to create keyframes. You are not going to be tweening from position to position like you did in the previous Bone Tool example. This will give the motion more of a robotic feel and be easier to sync with the tempo of the music.

1. Move the robot into a dance position for the 1st frame.

2. Select the next frame of each layer then add frames to them by selecting Insert ➤ Timeline ➤ Frame.

3. Now move the robot into a different dance position (remember the change in position will automatically create the keyframes).

4. Repeat steps 2 and 3 for the next 8 frames and you should end up with 10 frames of different dance positions.

5. Add a new layer (Insert ➤ Timeline ➤ Layer) above the others and name it *actions*, highlight frame 1 to frame 10, and add keyframes by selecting Modify ➤ Timeline ➤ Convert to Keyframes (F6).

6. Now open your Actions window by selecting Window ➤ Actions (Alt+F9/Option+F9) and add stop(); to frames 1–10.

7. Save your progress (Ctrl+S/Cmd+S).

That's it for the robot. Creating graphics for the room is the last step. It will be a simple room with a message board at the top of it (this will be needed for Chapter 4 when you learn about making widgets user configurable).

Drawing the Dance Floor and Message Board

Drawing the dance floor and message board is fairly straightforward. You will be using a new tool that I haven't discussed, but, in this case, its usage is very simple. Refer to Figure 3-5 for visual aid while doing the following steps.

1. Return to the main timeline, name the existing layer *robot*, add a new layer below this, and name it *room*. Temporarily hide the robot layer by clicking the dot below the eye symbol in the Timeline Window.

2. Select the Deco Tool (U) which looks like the pencil tool with a bunch of dots around it. In the Properties Window under the Drawing Effect section, select Grid Fill in the combo box.

3. Now click the top left portion of the stage which should draw a grid of black squares across the whole stage.

4. Select the grid and convert it to a movie clip with the name *floor*.

5. With this movie clip still selected, select the 3D Rotation Tool (W) and change the x axis by clicking down on the top part of the red vertical line and moving your cursor to the left until about 85 degrees is filled in the top left sector.

6. With the Selection Tool (V) drag the floor to the bottom of the stage. Notice as you drag it down, the angle changes. This is accounting for perspective which is automatic for objects that have been manipulated with the 3D Rotation Tool. The width and height should end up at about 780 x 150 pixels.

7. Using the Rectangle Tool (R), draw a 550 x 44 pixel, dark gray rectangle at the top of the stage. Now convert it to a movie clip with the name *messageBoard*.

8. Select this movie clip and click Edit ➤ Edit Symbols (Ctrl+E/Cmd+E) to enter its timeline. Again using the Rectangle Tool, draw a smaller, light gray rectangle within the other one, leaving a 4 pixel border on each side.

9. Use the Text Tool (T) to create a text field about the same size as the inner rectangle. In the Properties Window, select Dynamic Text in the first combo box and click the Align Center icon. Any font, color, and size will do (I used the *Good Times* font, a green color, and a 22pt size). Type in a message of your choice and give this text field an instance name of *message* so you can access it with ActionScript.

10. Return to the main timeline and give the message board you just created an instance name of *messageBoard*. Now add a Bevel Filter to it by

setting Blur X and Blur Y to 3, Strength to 50 percent, and Quality set to High.

11. Using the Line Tool (N), draw two vertical lines from the back two corners of the floor to the message board.

12. Save your progress (Ctrl+S/Cmd+S).

Figure 3-5. The completed room and message board.

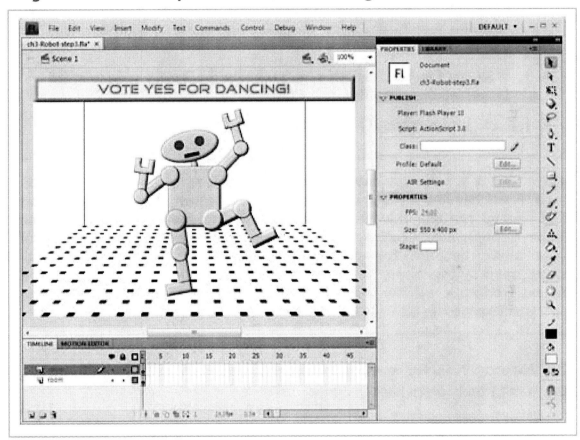

Importing the Music

Since you are finally done with the graphics, you can now import the music so the robot has something to dance to. You can use anything you would like, but shorter loops, rather than full length songs, would definitely be better for loading time. If you don't have any music, I've made a loop for you to use that can be downloaded at `www.createflashwidgets.com/book/loop.zip`. Once you have selected music, you can easily add it by doing the following.

1. In the main timeline, add a new layer and name it *sound*.

2. Click the 1st frame in that layer, select File ➤ Import ➤ Import to Stage (Ctrl+R/Cmd+R), and select the music file from your computer that you're going to use.

3. With that frame still selected, go to change the *Repeat* to *Loop* in the Sound section of the Properties Window.

4. Save your progress (Ctrl+S/Cmd+S).

Tip   It is better to import music into Flash as a wav file rather than mp3. Flash handles the compression and using other programs to convert files to mp3 can add unwanted time to the music, making it have a pause before it loops. Also, you may want to change the compression properties of your music because the default isn't too good. To do this, right-click/Ctrl+click the music file in the Library and select Properties. In the Sound Properties window that pops up, make sure Compression is set to *MP3* and change the Bit Rate to a higher value (*32 kbps* is what I used).

It's that easy. Now we're ready to start writing some ActionScript to make this robot finally learn how to dance.

Writing the Code

Writing the code in your example will be much less of a job than designing the graphics. All of your code will reside in one class which will be set as the Document Class of the movie. Start by selecting File ➤ New ➤

ActionScript File and save it as *Robot.as* in the same folder as *robot.fla*. Inside your script editor type the following:

```
package {

  import flash.events.*;
  import flash.display.MovieClip;
  import flash.utils.Timer;

  public class Robot extends MovieClip {

        private var numFrames:Number = 10;
        private var timerInterval:Number = 200;
        private var randomFrameTimer:Timer;

        private var maxX:Number = 230;
        private var minX:Number = 15;
        private var xChange:Number = 15;

        private var maxScale:Number = 1.2;
        private var minScale:Number = .7;
        private var scaleChange:Number = .05;

        public function Robot() {
            randomFrameTimer = new Timer(timerInterval);
            randomFrameTimer.addEventListener(TimerEvent.↪
TIMER,onTimer);
            randomFrameTimer.start();

    }

    private function onTimer(e:TimerEvent):void {
        //randomly pick the frame to change to
        var randomFrame = Math.round(Math.random() *↪
numFrames);
        //randomly move around the room
        switch(randomFrame) {
            case 1:
```

```
        case 2:
            //try to get him to move right
            if(robot.x <= maxX){
                robot.x += xChange;
            }else{
                robot.x -= xChange;
            }
        break;

        case 3:
        case 4:
            //try to get him to move left
            if(robot.x >= minX){
                robot.x -= xChange;
            }else{
                robot.x += xChange;
            }
         break;

    case 6:
    case 7:
        //try to get him to move backwards
        if(robot.scaleX >= minScale){
            robot.scaleX -= scaleChange;
            robot.scaleY -= scaleChange;
        }else{
            robot.scaleX += scaleChange;
            robot.scaleY += scaleChange;
        }
        break;

    case 8:
    case 9:
            //try to get him to move forward
          if(robot.scaleX <= maxScale){
              robot.scaleX += scaleChange;
              robot.scaleY += scaleChange;
          }else{
```

```
                    robot.scaleX -= scaleChange;
                    robot.scaleY -= scaleChange;
                }
                break;

            default:
                break;
        }
        //change to the random frame
        robot.gotoAndStop(randomFrame);
    }
  }
}
```

That is all the ActionScript you need to make your robot dance. Notice your class Robot extends the MovieClip class (remember this is necessary for all Document Classes). The property numFrames stores the number of frames you have set up dance positions in, and is used to set a limit when picking a random frame. The timeInterval property is the interval, in milliseconds, in which the timer event will be fired. You will definitely need to adjust this value based on the tempo of the music you chose. The bigger the number the slower the robot will dance. The randomFrameTimer is a Timer that can be set up to fire an event at a specified interval. The maxX, minX, maxScale, and minScale properties are used to limit the robot's motion and the xChange and scaleChange properties define the amount the robot moves left, right, backward, and forward.

The Robot function is the constructor of this class and is automatically called. All you do in this function is set up the randomFrameTimer property (setting its interval to the value of timerInterval), listen to the timer's event with the onTimer function, and start the timer. Within the onTimer function you start by picking a random number within the limits of numFrames. You then use a switch statement on this random number to determine whether the robot should move left, right, backward, or forward.

Within each case, you check to make sure the robot is still within bounds and if it is not, you move it in the opposite direction. You then use the random number again to move the robot's playhead to that frame in the Timeline. You end up with a robot that has countless random combinations of movements and dance positions, creating many possibilities to keep the viewer entertained.

Now the last thing you must do is open *robot.fla* and set the Class property (in the Properties Window of the stage) to *Robot*. This sets it as the Document Class and now you can test the movie and watch the robot dance.

For the Flash and ActionScript files discussed in this chapter, download `www.CreateFlashWidgets.com/book/robot.zip`.

Summary

In this chapter you designed your dancing robot, which incorporated the new tools you learned about in the previous chapter. You then brought the robot to life with some ActionScript, completing the basic functionality of your widget. In the next chapter, you will find out how to get the user more involved by making your widget user interactive and configurable. You will also learn how to use XML to drive your robot's dancing.

Chapter 4: Taking Flash Widgets to the Next Level

It is now time to find out about some other important aspects of widget development. The most essential of these is making your widget interactive. There are a few successful widgets that have no interaction, but for the most part it is a good idea to let your users get involved in some way. Allowing your widget to be configurable is also a good idea because this adds personalization, allowing users to end up with slight differences and making them feel like your widget is more their own. You can also drive your widget with XML, separating some of the data from the Flash movie, which opens up many possibilities. You will find out how to incorporate each of these things with the robot example we created in the previous chapter.

Adding Interactivity

Without interaction, most widgets just wouldn't work. For the most part, widget users want to be able to create an effect, whether it's by clicking on a cat to make it meow or playing a fully interactive game. The few non-interactive widgets that do work are mostly informational widgets, like baby-birth counters or news feeds. These are very popular and are usually just visually pleasing or creative ways to show information. There are many different ways to make the widget interactive, but it all comes down to actions taken by the mouse and the keyboard. Mouse-over, mouse-out, mouse-up, mouse-down, mouse-move, keyboard-up, and keyboard-down are the triggers available for interaction. With these you can activate buttons, make objects draggable, control movie clips with the keyboard arrows, and create custom cursors, etc. The important thing to keep in mind when adding interactivity to your widget is to stay simple. A complex set of interactions or interactions that are not intuitive can easily drive potential users away.

For the widget example, you will first be adding mouse-over and mouse-out states so the robot won't dance and the music won't sound until the cursor is over the movie clip. You will also be making your widget pause and play when users click on it.

Mouse-Over and Mouse-Out States

While the cursor isn't over your widget, you'll silence the music (so as not to annoy the user) and put the robot in a deactivated position, with the hands down and eyes closed. When the user gets curious and rolls over your widget with his mouse, the music will start and the robot will activate (start dancing). When the user is done and rolls back off the movie, everything will stop and the robot will again deactivate. First, you'll take up the graphic changes and then the ActionScript additions.

1. Start by opening the *robot.fla* and *Robot.as* files you worked on in the previous chapter.

2. In *robot.fla*, select the robot and click Edit ➤ Edit Symbols (Ctrl+E/Cmd+E) to enter its timeline. Add a new layer and name it *labels*.

3. Click the 11th Frame of this layer and select Insert ➤ Timeline ➤ Keyframe. Click on this keyframe and name it *asleep* in the Label section of the Properties Window.

4. Add an additional frame to the remaining layers by selecting frame 11 of each and clicking Insert ➤ Timeline ➤ Frame (F5).

5. One by one, click on the layers containing the left leg, right leg, left arm, and right arm and straighten out each so they are lifeless and pointing toward the floor (as shown in Figure 4-1).

6. Select the head of the robot and click Edit ➤ Edit Symbols (Ctrl+E/Cmd+E) to enter its timeline. Then select one of the eyes and

click Edit ➤ Edit Symbols (Ctrl+E/Cmd+E). Within this timeline, add a new layer (Insert ➤ Timeline ➤ Layer) and name it *actions*.

7. Then select the 2nd frame and add a keyframe by clicking Insert ➤ Timeline ➤ Keyframe. Type stop(); in the Actions Window for both the 1st and 2nd keyframe of this layer.

8. Now add another new layer (Insert ➤ Timeline ➤ Layer) and name it *labels*. Then select the 2nd frame and add a keyframe by clicking Insert ➤ Timeline ➤ Keyframe.

9. Next select the 1st keyframe and name it *awake* and select the 2nd keyframe and name it *asleep*.

Figure 4-1. The lifeless state of the robot when the user's mouse is not over the movie.

10. You should now have three layers. Rename the remaining layer containing the eye, *graphics*, and select the 2nd frame. Then add a keyframe by clicking Insert ➤ Timeline ➤ Keyframe.

11. Click on this newly created keyframe and select the center of the eye and change its color to black. Then select the whole eye (including the outline) and use the Free Transform Tool (Q) to make it into a squinting-eye shape.

12. Now return to the main timeline and create a new layer (Insert ➤ Timeline ➤ Layer) above all the other graphic layers and name it *cover*. Click on the 1st frame of this layer and use the Rectangle Tool (R) to draw a rectangle the size of the stage. Select it and convert it to a movie clip with the name *cover* by clicking Modify ➤ Convert to Symbol.

13. Now in the Properties Window, give it an instance name of *cover* and under the Color Effect section select Alpha and enter in a value of 0 to make it invisible.

14. Save your progress (Ctrl+S/Cmd+S).

Those are all the changes you need to make with regard to the graphics. Now you need to add a couple new properties and functions to the Robot class to turn the robot and the music on and off. In order to control the music you will need to instantiate it with ActionScript instead of embedding it on the Timeline. So before you start writing the new code you will need to do these quick steps:

1. Go to the main timeline and delete the sound layer.

2. Open the Library, right-click (Ctrl+click) on the sound, and select Properties. Now click the Advanced button and select the Export for ActionScript checkbox. Type in *Loop* as the class and press the OK button. (You will get an ActionScript warning saying the class does not exist. Click OK because Flash will create the class for you. You are just assigning a class to this so you can access it through ActionScript.)

You are now ready to make your changes and additions to the Robot class. Open *Robot.as* and make the following changes.

```
package {

import flash.events.*;
import flash.display.MovieClip;
import flash.utils.Timer;
import flash.media.*;


public class Robot extends MovieClip {

    private var numFrames:Number = 10;
    private var timerInterval:Number = 200;
    private var randomFrameTimer:Timer;

    private var maxX:Number = 230;
    private var minX:Number = 15;
    private var xChange:Number = 15;

    private var maxScale:Number = 1.2;
    private var minScale:Number = .7;
    private var scaleChange:Number = .05;

    private var music:Loop;
    private var soundChannel:SoundChannel;


    public function Robot() {
        music = new Loop();

        randomFrameTimer = new Timer(timerInterval);
        randomFrameTimer.addEventListener(↵
TimerEvent.TIMER,onTimer);
        //notice we removed randomFrameTimer.start();
        //set initial robot state
        robot.buttonMode = true;
        robot.gotoAndStop("asleep");
        robot.head.rightEye.gotoAndStop("asleep");
        robot.head.leftEye.gotoAndStop("asleep");
```

```
            //events which handle the activation and↪
deactivation of the robot
        cover.addEventListener(↪
MouseEvent.MOUSE_OVER, onMouseOver);
        cover.addEventListener(MouseEvent.MOUSE_OUT,↪
onMouseOut);
    }

    private function onMouseOver(e:MouseEvent):void{
        activate();
    }
    private function onMouseOut(e:MouseEvent):void{
        deactivate();
    }
    private function deactivate():void{
        robot.gotoAndStop("asleep");
        robot.head.rightEye.gotoAndStop("asleep");
        robot.head.leftEye.gotoAndStop("asleep");
        randomFrameTimer.stop();
        soundChannel.stop();
    }
    private function activate():void{
        robot.head.rightEye.gotoAndStop("awake");
        robot.head.leftEye.gotoAndStop("awake");
        randomFrameTimer.start();
        soundChannel = music.play(0,int.MAX_VALUE);
    }


    private function onTimer(e:TimerEvent):void {
        //randomly pick the frame to change to
        var randomFrame = Math.round(Math.random() *↪
numFrames);
        //randomly move around the room
        switch(randomFrame){
            case 1:
            case 2:
                //try to get him to move right
```

```
                if(robot.x <= maxX){
                    robot.x += xChange;
                }else{
                    robot.x -= xChange;
                }
            break;

            case 3:
            case 4:
                    //try to get him to move left
                if(robot.x >= minX){
                    robot.x -= xChange;
                }else{
                    robot.x += xChange;
                }
              break;

        case 6:
        case 7:
            //try to get him to move backwards
                if(robot.scaleX >= minScale){
                robot.scaleX -= scaleChange;
                robot.scaleY -= scaleChange;
            }else{
                robot.scaleX += scaleChange;
                    robot.scaleY += scaleChange;
            }
            break;

        case 8:
        case 9:
            //try to get him to move forward
              if(robot.scaleX <= maxScale){
                    robot.scaleX += scaleChange;
                robot.scaleY += scaleChange;
            }else{
                robot.scaleX -= scaleChange;
                robot.scaleY -= scaleChange;
```

```
                }
            break;

                default:
                    break;
            }
            //change to the random frame
            robot.gotoAndStop(randomFrame);
        }
    }
}
```

In the code, you add two new properties: music, which is an instance of the
Loop class that is automatically created by Flash for the sound in the
Library and soundChannel, which is used to stop music when the robot is
deactivated. In the constructor function, you add the instantiation of music,
set the buttonMode property of robot to *true* (activating the hand cursor on
roll over), set the robot to sleep mode, and add the mouse-over and mouse-
out events to cover. The reason you add these events to cover rather than
stage is that your widget, in some cases, will be wrapped by another SWF
that prevents calls to stage. The onMouseOver and onMouseOut functions
that handle these events simply call activate and deactivate
respectively. The deactivate function sets the robot to sleep mode, stops
the timer that makes it dance, and also stops the music. The activate
function turns the robot on, starts the timer to make it dance, and starts the
music. That's all you've added to the *Robot.as* class. Save it and test the
movie to check out the additions. Isn't it nice to have some control over
your widget? Well, you're about to add a bit more control by adding
mouse-click functionality and a response to the mouse as it changes
position.

Handling the Mouse-Click Event and Cursor Position

You'll be using the same `activate` and `deactivate` functions for the mouse-click event; you'll just need to add a listener to `cover`. Instead of moving the robot randomly around the room, you are going to make it so the user can guide it with the cursor position. To do this, you will need to make a few changes to the `onTimer` function that causes the robot to move based on its x and y in relation to the mouse x and y. Make the following changes to *Robot.as*:

```
package {

import flash.events.*;
import flash.display.MovieClip;
import flash.utils.Timer;
import flash.media.*;

public class Robot extends MovieClip {

    private var numFrames:Number = 10;
    private var timerInterval:Number = 200;
    private var randomFrameTimer:Timer;

    private var maxX:Number = 230;
    private var minX:Number = 15;
    private var xChange:Number = 15;

    private var maxScale:Number = 1.2;
    private var minScale:Number = .7;
    private var scaleChange:Number = .05;

    private var music:Loop;
    private var soundChannel:SoundChannel;

    private var mode:String;
```

```
    public function Robot() {
        music = new Loop();
        randomFrameTimer = new Timer(timerInterval);
        randomFrameTimer.addEventListener(↪
TimerEvent.TIMER,onTimer);
        //notice we removed randomFrameTimer.start();
        //set initial robot state
        robot.buttonMode = true;

        robot.gotoAndStop("asleep");
        robot.head.rightEye.gotoAndStop("asleep");
        robot.head.leftEye.gotoAndStop("asleep");

        mode = "deactivated";

        //events which handle the activation and↪
deactivation of the robot
        cover.addEventListener(↪
MouseEvent.MOUSE_OVER, onMouseOver);
        cover.addEventListener(MouseEvent.MOUSE_OUT,↪
onMouseOut);

            cover.addEventListener(MouseEvent.CLICK,↪
onMouseClick);
    }

    private function onMouseClick(e:MouseEvent):void {
        if(mode=="activated"){
            deactivate();
        }else{
            activate();
        }
    }
    private function onMouseOver(e:MouseEvent):void{
        activate();
    }
    private function onMouseOut(e:MouseEvent):void{
        deactivate();
    }
```

```
private function deactivate():void{

    mode = "deactivated";

    robot.gotoAndStop("asleep");
    robot.head.rightEye.gotoAndStop("asleep");
    robot.head.leftEye.gotoAndStop("asleep");
    randomFrameTimer.stop();
    soundChannel.stop();
}
private function activate():void{

    mode = "activated";

    robot.head.rightEye.gotoAndStop("awake");
    robot.head.leftEye.gotoAndStop("awake");
    randomFrameTimer.start();
    soundChannel = music.play(0,int.MAX_VALUE);
}

private function onTimer(e:TimerEvent):void {
    //randomly pick the frame to change to
    var randomFrame = Math.round(Math.random() *➥
numFrames);
    //change to the random frame
    robot.gotoAndStop(randomFrame);


    //react to mouse position
    var robotX:Number = robot.x+(robot.width/2);
    var robotY:Number = robot.y+(robot.width/2);
    //x change
    if(cover.mouseX > robotX){
            //try to get him to move right
        if(robot.x <= maxX){
            robot.x += xChange;
        }
    }else if(cover.mouseX < robotX){
            //try to get him to move left
        if(robot.x >= minX){
            robot.x -= xChange;
```

```
            }
        }
        //scale change
        if(cover.mouseY > robotY){
            //try to get him to move backwards
                if(robot.scaleX <= maxScale){
                robot.scaleX += scaleChange;
                robot.scaleY += scaleChange;
            }
          }else if(cover.mouseY < robotY){
            //try to get him to move forward
                if(robot.scaleX >= minScale){
                    robot.scaleX -= scaleChange;
                robot.scaleY -= scaleChange;
            }
        }
    }

    }
  }
}
```

To have click functionality, first you add mode, a property that keeps track
of whether the robot is activated or deactivated. You set this to
"deactivated" in the constructor and add a mouse-click event to cover. The
handler for this, onMouseClick, checks mode and calls activate or
deactivate to switch its state. You also set mode in the activate and
deactivate functions. To make the robot move around the room based on
the cursor position, you add two new variables, robotX and robotY, which
represent the center of the robot. Then you check to see if the cursor's x
position is greater or less than robotX and try (checking against minX and
maxX) to move the robot right or left accordingly. Finally, you do the same
comparison with the cursor's y position and robotY, but instead of its y
property you alter the robot's scale, moving him back and forth. Save the
class and test the movie to check out the changes.

Now you have an interactive robot that can be turned off and on by clicking and also guided around the room with the cursor. This gets the user more involved and makes your widget more interesting and fun. Next you will be making your widget more personalized by adding a configuration for users.

Making It Configurable

There are many configurations you can do with this robot, given some changes, such as letting the user choose different style body parts, colors, or music. To keep it simple while still getting the basic idea, you'll be making the text of the message board configurable. Configurations work with widgets through parameters passed to the Flash movie. These parameters can be passed in multiple ways but the simplest way is using a query string, like movie.swf?var1=123. If you're not familiar with this, the target is movie.swf and the question mark signifies that variables are being passed to the target. var1 is the name of the example parameter and 123 is the example value. To get this parameter in your Flash movie, you'll need to access the loaderInfo property of the MovieClip class, which your Robot class extends. Through this property you can access the parameters sent to your widget. Since the message text is now configurable, you'll also need to handle text which is longer than the width of the message board. To do this, you'll check if the text is too long and if it is, you'll make it scroll. To make these changes you will not need to alter *robot.fla* but only make the following changes to *Robot.as*.

```
package {

import flash.events.*;
import flash.display.MovieClip;
import flash.utils.Timer;
import flash.media.*;
import flash.text.*;


public class Robot extends MovieClip {
```

```
private var numFrames:Number = 10;
private var timerInterval:Number = 200;
private var randomFrameTimer:Timer;

private var maxX:Number = 230;
private var minX:Number = 15;
private var xChange:Number = 15;

private var maxScale:Number = 1.2;
private var minScale:Number = .7;
private var scaleChange:Number = .05;

private var music:Loop;
private var soundChannel:SoundChannel;

private var mode:String;
private var defaultMessage:String = "Vote Yes For↪
Dancing!";


public function Robot() {
    this.loaderInfo.addEventListener(↪
Event.COMPLETE, onSWFLoaded);
    music = new Loop();
    randomFrameTimer = new Timer(timerInterval);
    randomFrameTimer.addEventListener(↪
TimerEvent.TIMER, onTimer);
    //notice we removed randomFrameTimer.start();
    //set initial robot state
    robot.buttonMode = true;
     robot.gotoAndStop("asleep");
     robot.head.rightEye.gotoAndStop("asleep");
    robot.head.leftEye.gotoAndStop("asleep");
    mode = "deactivated";
```

```
        //events which handle the activation and⮯
deactivation of the robot
        cover.addEventListener(⮯
MouseEvent.MOUSE_OVER, onMouseOver);
        cover.addEventListener(MouseEvent.MOUSE_OUT,⮯
onMouseOut);
        cover.addEventListener(MouseEvent.CLICK,⮯
onMouseClick);
    }


    private function onSWFLoaded(e:Event):void{
        this.loaderInfo.removeEventListener(⮯
Event.COMPLETE, onSWFLoaded);
        var queryString:Object =⮯
this.loaderInfo.parameters;
        if(queryString.message != null){
                messageBoard.message.text =⮯
queryString.message;
        }else{
                messageBoard.message.text =⮯
defaultMessage;
        }
        checkTextWidth();
    }
    private function checkTextWidth():void{
        var mbTW:Number=messageBoard.message.textWidth;
        var mbW:Number=messageBoard.message.width;
        if(mbTW > mbW){
            setupScrollingText();
        }
    }

    private function setupScrollingText():void {
        //draw mask for text
        var tbX:Number=messageBoard.textBackground.x;
        var tbY:Number=messageBoard.textBackground.y;
```

```
            var tbW:Number=↪
messageBoard.textBackground.width;
            var tbH:Number=↪
messageBoard.textBackground.height;

        var textMask:MovieClip = new MovieClip();
        textMask.graphics.lineStyle(1);
        textMask.graphics.beginFill(0xFFFFFF);
        textMask.graphics.lineTo(tbW,0);
        textMask.graphics.lineTo(tbW, tbH);
        textMask.graphics.lineTo(0, tbH);
        textMask.graphics.lineTo(0, 0);
        textMask.graphics.endFill();
        messageBoard.addChild(textMask);
        textMask.x = tbX;
        textMask.y = tbY;


        //setup mask
        messageBoard.message.mask = textMask;
        messageBoard.message.autoSize =↪
TextFieldAutoSize.LEFT;
        messageBoard.message.x = tbW;

        //setup timer for movement
        var textTimer:Timer = new Timer(13);
        textTimer.addEventListener( TimerEvent.TIMER,↪
onTextTimer);
        textTimer.start();
    }

    private function onTextTimer(e:TimerEvent):void{
        var tbX:Number=messageBoard.textBackground.x;
        var tbW:Number=↪
messageBoard.textBackground.width;
        var mbX:Number=messageBoard.message.x;
        var mbW:Number=messageBoard.message.width;
```

```
    //move text
    messageBoard.message.x -= 1;
    //check if off screen
    if(mbX + mbW < tbX){
        messageBoard.message.x = tbW;
    }
  }
}
```

Keep the rest of the file as is. In the previous code, you add a new property to the class `defaultMessage` and give it a default value in case no configuration is made by the user. In the constructor function, you add an event listener to call a function when the SWF has finished loading. This function, `onSWFLoaded`, checks a parameter that will be sent to the Flash movie and sets it as the message board text. If the parameter is not there, the default message is used. You then call `checkTextWidth`, a function that uses the `width` property (width of the text field) and `textWidth` property (width of the text within the text field) to check if it needs to be scrolled. If it does, you call `setupScrollingText`, which draws a mask for the text and sets up a timer to continuously call `onTextTimer`. This function scrolls the text by changing its x property and resets the text's x property if it has scrolled off screen. Save the class and test the movie (if you want to test the scrolling, just make your default message something longer than the message board).

The actual configuration portion of this will be done in the next chapter because it is not a change in the code but rather a setting at WidgetBox.com. Before that you'll be exploring the use of an external XML file with your widget.

Driving It with XML

With XML you can do many useful things with widgets. For example, if you were making a movie trivia widget, it would be a good idea to separate the questions and answers from the Flash file. This would make it easier to add questions and make it so users could also contribute their own. Instead of having to manually add questions and recompile the FLA, you could have a script that writes them to your XML and your current SWF all of a sudden has additional content. With the robot, you'll be choreographing his dances with lists of numbers stored in an XML file. The numbers will represent each frame (dance move) to go to and they will be repeated. Each time the robot stops then starts again, you'll select a random dance pattern to change it up a bit. You'll start with the XML, which will be extremely simple for this example. Open a text editor such as Notepad and type the following:

```
<dances count="3">
    <dance id="1">1,3,2,3,2,4,1,4,3,1,2,1,5</dance>
    <dance id="2">5,6,5,6,7,8,7,8,9,8,7,6,5</dance>
    <dance id="3">10,8,4,10,8,4,1,2,3,1,2,3</dance>
</dances>
```

Now save this file as *dances.xml* in the same directory as *robot.fla* and *Robot.as*. You have created three dances that you can load into your widget to guide the robot. Feel free to change the numbers around however you wish.

Next we need to set up our Robot class to load this XML file and read it. To accomplish this, make the following changes to *Robot.as:*

```
package {

import flash.display.MovieClip;
import flash.utils.Timer;
import flash.events.*;
import flash.media.*;
import flash.text.*;

import flash.xml.*;
import flash.net.*;


public class Robot extends MovieClip {
```

```
    private var numFrames:Number = 10;
    private var timerInterval:Number = 220;
    private var randomFrameTimer:Timer;

    private var maxX:Number = 230;
    private var minX:Number = 15;
    private var xChange:Number = 15;

    private var maxScale:Number = 1.2;
    private var minScale:Number = .7;
    private var scaleChange:Number = .05;

    private var music:Loop;
    private var soundChannel:SoundChannel;

    private var mode:String;
    private var defaultMessage = "Vote Yes For↪
Dancing!";

    private var xmlFile:String = "dances.xml";
    private var xml:XML;

    private var randomDancing:Boolean=false;

    private var numDances:Number;
    private var currentDance:Number;

    private var dancePattern:Array;
    private var patternPosition:Number;


    public function Robot () {
        this.loaderInfo.addEventListener(↪
Event.COMPLETE, onSWFLoaded);
        //check to see if we should load the xml or↪
just do some random dancing

        if(randomDancing==false){
```

```
                loadXML();
        }else {
            init();
        }
    }
    private function init():void {
        music = new Loop();

        randomFrameTimer=new Timer(timerInterval);
        randomFrameTimer.addEventListener(➥
TimerEvent.TIMER, onTimer);
        //set initial robot state
        robot.buttonMode = true;

        robot.gotoAndStop("asleep");
        robot.head.rightEye.gotoAndStop("asleep");
        robot.head.leftEye.gotoAndStop("asleep");
        mode="deactivated";
        //events which handle the activation and➥
deactivation of the robot
        cover.addEventListener(MouseEvent.MOUSE_OVER,➥
onMouseOver);
        cover.addEventListener(MouseEvent.MOUSE_OUT,➥
onMouseOut);
        cover.addEventListener(MouseEvent.CLICK,➥
onMouseClick);
    }


    private function loadXML():void{
        var xmlLoader:URLLoader = new URLLoader();
        xmlLoader.addEventListener(Event.COMPLETE,➥
onXMLLoaded);
        xmlLoader.addEventListener(➥
IOErrorEvent.IO_ERROR, onXMLError);
        xmlLoader.load(new URLRequest(xmlFile));
    }
```

```actionscript
    private function onXMLLoaded(e:Event):void {
        xml = new XML(e.target.data);
        //check how many dances are available
        numDances = Number(xml.attribute("count"));
        init();
    }

    private function onXMLError(e:IOErrorEvent):void {
        trace("XML Load Error: "+e);
    }

    private function pickDance():void {
        //set current dance within the range of↪
numDances
        currentDance = Math.floor ( Math.random() *↪
numDances +1 );
        //get dance whose id matches currentDance
        var danceList:String =↪
xml.dance.(@id==currentDance);
        //convert string to array
        dancePattern = danceList.split(",");
        //reset patternPosition
        patternPosition = 0;
    }


    private function onSWFLoaded(e:Event):void{
        var queryString = this.loaderInfo.parameters;
        if(queryString.message != null){
            messageBoard.message.text =↪
queryString.message;
        }else{
            messageBoard.message.text = defaultMessage;
        }
        checkTextWidth();
        this.loaderInfo.removeEventListener(↪
Event.COMPLETE, onSWFLoaded);
    }
```

```
    private function checkTextWidth():void{
        var mbTW:Number=messageBoard.message.textWidth;
        var mbW:Number=messageBoard.message.width;
        if(mbTW > mbW){
            setupScrollingText();
        }
    }

    private function setupScrollingText():void {
        //draw mask for text
        var tbX:Number=messageBoard.textBackground.x;
        var tbY:Number=messageBoard.textBackground.y;
        var tbW:Number=➥
messageBoard.textBackground.width;
        var tbH:Number=➥
messageBoard.textBackground.height;

        var textMask:MovieClip = new MovieClip();
        textMask.graphics.lineStyle(1);
        textMask.graphics.beginFill(0xFFFFFF);
        textMask.graphics.lineTo(tbW,0);
        textMask.graphics.lineTo(tbW, tbH);
        textMask.graphics.lineTo(0, tbH);
        textMask.graphics.lineTo(0, 0);
        textMask.graphics.endFill();
        messageBoard.addChild(textMask);
        textMask.x = tbX;
        textMask.y = tbY;


        //setup mask
        messageBoard.message.mask = textMask;
        messageBoard.message.autoSize =➥
TextFieldAutoSize.LEFT;
        messageBoard.message.x = tbW;

        //setup timer for movement
```

```
        var textTimer:Timer = new Timer(13);
        textTimer.addEventListener(TimerEvent.TIMER,↪
onTextTimer);
        textTimer.start();
    }

    private function onTextTimer(e:TimerEvent):void{
        var tbX:Number=messageBoard.textBackground.x;
        var tbW:Number=↪
messageBoard.textBackground.width;
        var mbX:Number=messageBoard.message.x;
        var mbW:Number=messageBoard.message.width;
        //move text
        messageBoard.message.x -= 1;
        //check if off screen
        if(mbX + mbW < tbX){
            messageBoard.message.x = tbW;
        }
    }

    private function onMouseClick (e:MouseEvent):void{
        if(mode == "activated"){
            deactivate();
        }else{
            activate();
        }
    }

    private function onMouseOver(e:MouseEvent):void{
        activate();
    }

    private function onMouseOut(e:MouseEvent):void{
        deactivate();
    }

    private function deactivate():void{
        mode = "deactivated";
```

```
        robot.gotoAndStop("asleep");
        robot.head.rightEye.gotoAndStop("asleep");
        robot.head.leftEye.gotoAndStop("asleep");
        randomFrameTimer.stop();
        soundChannel.stop();
    }

    private function activate():void{
        mode = "activated";
        robot.head.rightEye.gotoAndStop("awake");
        robot.head.leftEye.gotoAndStop("awake");

        if(randomDancing == false){
            pickDance();
        }

        randomFrameTimer.start();
        soundChannel = music.play(0, int.MAX_VALUE);
    }

    private function onTimer(e:TimerEvent):void {

        if(randomDancing==false){
        //make sure patternPosition is not out of range
            if(!dancePattern[patternPosition]){
                //if it is reset patternPosition
                patternPosition=0;
            }
            //change to next value in dancePattern
            robot.gotoAndStop(↪
dancePattern[patternPosition]);
            patternPosition++;
        }else{
            //randomly pick the frame to change to
            var randomFrame = Math.round(↪
Math.random() * numFrames);
            //change to the random frame
            robot.gotoAndStop(randomFrame);
```

```actionscript
		}

		//react to mouse position
		var robotX:Number = robot.x+(robot.width/2);
		var robotY:Number = robot.y+(robot.width/2);
		//x change
		if(cover.mouseX > robotX){
			//try to get him to move right
			if(robot.x <= maxX){
				robot.x += xChange;
			}
		}else if(cover.mouseX < robotX){
			//try to get him to move left
			if(robot.x >= minX){
				robot.x -= xChange;
			}
		}
		//scale change
		if(cover.mouseY > robotY){
			//try to get him to move backwards
			if(robot.scaleX <= maxScale){
				robot.scaleX += scaleChange;
				robot.scaleY += scaleChange;
			}
		}else if(cover.mouseY < robotY){
			//try to get him to move forward
			 if(robot.scaleX >= minScale){
				robot.scaleX -= scaleChange;
				 robot.scaleY -= scaleChange;
			}
		}
	}
	}
}
}
```

In the preceding code, first you import two new packages, `flash.xml` and `flash.net`. You then add several new class properties: `xmlFile`, which is the name of the XML file that is loaded; `xml`, which holds the content of this file; `randomDancing`, which you use to turn off and on the usage of XML; `numDances`, which is the total number of dances provided in the XML file; `currentDance`, which keeps track of which dance pattern is being used (matches the `id` attribute of the `dance` element); `dancePattern`, which stores the array of frame numbers included in the dance; and `patternPosition`, which is the current index of `dancePattern`.

You then take most of the code in the constructor function and put it in a new function, `init`. This is so the robot doesn't automatically start, so you can check `randomDancing` in the constructor and see if you need to first load the XML. The `loadXML` function simply sets up `xmlLoader` to load `xmlFile` and adds some event listeners to know when it's done or has encountered an error. When it is done `onXMLLoaded` is called, which sets `xml` with the contents of the file and sets `numDances` with the `count` attribute of the main element. You then call `init` to proceed as you normally do. Now the only two differences left are when the robot is activated: First, `pickDance` is called, which selects a random dance from `xml` and sets it to `dancePattern`. Second, in `onTimer` you check `randomDancing` to see if you should pick a random frame or use the `patternPosition` to get the next frame from `dancePattern`. Save the class and test the movie to see your choreographed dances in action.

There are many more things you can do with this, such as assigning each dance a different piece of music and tempo or making it so users can create and save their own dances. Both of these wouldn't be too hard to accomplish but would definitely be big enough changes to convolute the purpose of this example. Plus, there is still quite a bit to go over. Now is a good time to make any finishing touches to your widget, like adding graphics to the robot's torso, coloring the walls of the room, etc. Or, if you're eager to go on and find out how to publish it, you can leave it as is.

Summary

In this chapter, you made the widget interactive, giving the user the ability to start, stop, and guide the robot around the room. You also set up the robot to be able to receive a configurable property from the user. Then you created an external XML file that you loaded and read at runtime to control the robot's dancing. All three of these are very important things to know when it comes to widget development. In the next chapter, you'll be learning how to get the widget on the Internet and manage it with WidgetBox.com.

Chapter 5: Publishing, Promoting, and Capitalizing on Your Widgets

Now that you're done creating your example widget, you are ready to get it out on as many outlets as possible. There are quite a few steps to get this done but each one is fairly simple. You will first need to get your widget up on a server then sign up with WidgetBox. You will then get familiar with this web site and setup, test, and publish your widget. This will allow people to find it on WidgetBox and get the embed code to paste in a personal site, blog, or editable profile page. Next, you'll need to take the steps to make your widget available on various social-networking sites. Finally, you'll look into ways to promote and potentially make money off your widgets.

The Prerequisites

Before you can make your widget available to the public, you must make one quick change to the code and put it up on a server. If you already have web hosting setup then you're good to go, but for those of you who don't, let's go over some options. You also need to join WidgetBox so you can add your widget and learn everything there is to know about this extremely helpful web site.

Setting Up the Server

Though there are many different web hosts with various plan types, you just need a simple one. I recommend paying for a highly-rated, inexpensive web hosting solution like HostGator.com or BlueHost.com. HostGator is cheaper but BlueHost gives you a free domain for the life of the hosting account when you sign up. Another option that is free but tedious to sign up for is X10Hosting.com. My advice is to spend a little cash and get hosting that won't drive you nuts.

Setting Up the Domain Name

If you don't go with web hosting that gives you a domain with your account, you have two options: use an "Access Domain" or purchase a domain. An *access* domain is a domain, provided by web hosting companies, that points to your web site. For a web site that people will actually be visiting this isn't a good option because of the awkwardness of the domain. But it is sufficient for what we're doing because the domain is only used to access the files being stored (no one will actually be going to the site). The best part about this option is it's free. If you want to purchase a domain name, most web-hosting sites will provide domain registration. If you end up with one that doesn't, Godaddy.com is one of the most popular domain registration sites. Once you have your domain, you'll need to point it to the DNS (Domain Name Server) of your web hosting. This can usually be found in the control panel of your hosting account under DNS information and will look something like this: "ns1.yourhosting.net."

Getting Your Widget Ready to Deploy

Before you upload your widget to the Internet, you need to make sure you change all relative paths to absolute. This is necessary because your SWF is not running from your own site. In your case, you only have one: *dances.xml*. So open *Robot.as* and change the existing line:

```
private var xmlFile:String = "dances.xml";
```

to the following:

```
private var xmlFile:String = "http://www.your-
domain.com/dances.xml";
```

Make sure you replace "www.your-domain.com" with your actual domain name or access domain.

Uploading the Files

Once this is done, we'll need to upload your files to this server. This will include robot.*swf*, *dances.xml*, and a cross-domain policy file that allows your SWF, when it is loaded by other servers, to access files on your server (in this case *dances.xml*). This file is simple to create, just open up Notepad and type the following:

```
<?xml version="1.0"?>
<!DOCTYPE cross-domain-policy SYSTEM
"http://www.adobe.com/xml/dtds/cross-domain-policy.dtd">

<cross-domain-policy>
        <site-control permitted-cross-domain-↵
policies="master-only"/>
        <allow-access-from domain="*"/>
        <allow-http-request-headers-from domain="*"
headers="*"/>
</cross-domain-policy>
```

Now save this file as *crossdomain.xml*. The "*" is giving permission to a SWF running on any domain to access the files on your server. In some cases, this may not be desirable or secure but for what you're doing it is not a problem and necessary if you want your widget to work anywhere it is installed. To find out more about cross-domain policy files, go to `http://www.adobe.com/devnet/articles/crossdomain_policy_file_spec.html`.

To upload these three files, you can use an FTP program, such as FlashFXP (a demo can be downloaded at `http://flashfxp.com/download.php`) or use the FTP solution in the control panel of your web-hosting account. This is all you need to do on your server, now you can sign up with WidgetBox.

Signing Up with WidgetBox

You can access all the widgets on WidgetBox without signing up, but in order to add your own, you'll need to become a member. This doesn't cost a thing and it is very simple. Just go to `http://www.widgetbox.com` (shown in Figure 5-1), click the Join Now link at the top-right of the page, fill out the form that pops up, and you're done.

Figure 5-1. The home page of the WidgetBox web site. This is where you can find the newest, featured, and all time favorite widgets. You can also search or browse by category to find specific widgets. From this page you have quick access to your own widgets with the My Widgetbox tab.

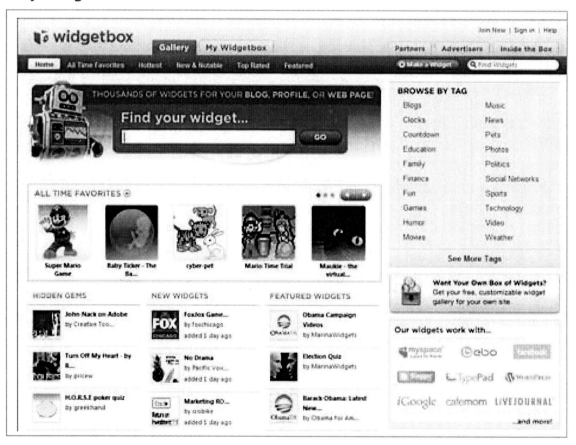

Now let's get familiar with this site before you continue. Return to the home page and click on one of the widgets in the "All Time Favorites" section. This takes you to a page, like the one shown in Figure 5-2, which lets you test the widget, customize it, install it, read comments and ratings about it, and get information about its developer. Every widget you submit will automatically get a page like this one. Click the Get Widget button, near the top-right of the page and a box will pop up that gives you the widget's embed code and ways to add it to various sites. Click the Copy button to copy the code to your clipboard and now you can paste this in one of your web sites, blogs, or social profiles. Close this box and click the My WidgetBox tab at the top-middle of the page. You should now be on a page that displays the widget you just copied the embed code for. All widgets you install and develop can be accessed through this page. That is all you need to know but feel free to continue exploring the Widgetbox site before going on to the next section.

Figure 5-2. The type of page that every submitted widget gets embedded in. Notice the customizations on the right side for this particular widget. You can change the type of animal, name, color, the adopter's name, and the size of the widget.

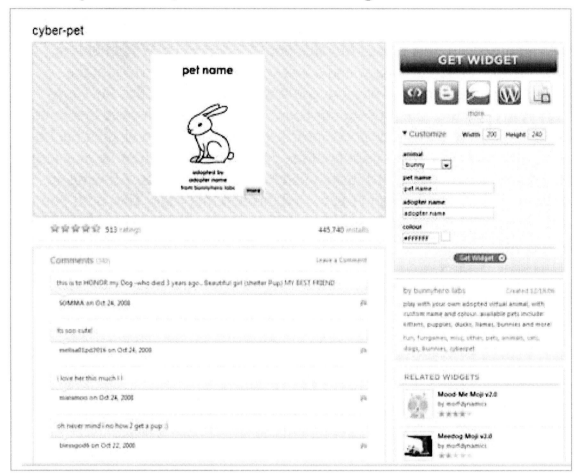

Adding Your Widget

To begin the process of adding your widget to WidgetBox, click the Make a Widget button near the top-right area of the web site. This will take you to a page like the one shown in Figure 5-3. On this page you can select the type of widget you are making, which in your case is, of course, Flash.

Once you've selected this, two input boxes will pop up below—one for the Flash Code or URL of your SWF and the other for the name of your widget. In the first input box type "`http://www.your-domain.com/robot.swf`" (replacing "your-domain" with your actual domain name or access domain) and in the second type "Dancing Robot" or whatever you would like to name it. Then press the Continue button on the bottom-right to go to the next step.

Figure 5-3. The page where you begin the process of making a new widget. Notice the other types of widgets you can make with Widgetbox.

On the next page, you can preview and customize the settings of your widget. Start by reading over the Developer Agreement and checking the box that indicates you have done so. Now ensure your widget is functioning properly in the Preview section. If it is not, you may have forgotten to upload *crossdomain.xml* or *dances.xml* to your server.

TIP   To troubleshoot your widget not working properly, type its URL in a browser, and if it works, it is probably a missing or malformed *crossdomain.xml*. If it still doesn't work, it is probably a missing *dances.xml* or a problem with the path to *dances.xml*.

Next, look at the Widget Settings section and notice that the Width and Height properties are filled in correctly (this is automatic). Now click the Add New Setting button. This pops up a window that allows you to configure your custom setting. You are going to use this setting for your configurable message board. The first input in this window, Setting Label, will be what the user sees when configuring your widget. Since this is a configuration for the message board text, set this property to *Message*. The

Param Name property will have to match what you are checking in the onSWFLoaded function of your Robot class; so set it to *message*. Keep the Flash Mode set to *Query String* and the Type set to *Text Field*. Set the Help Text property to *The displayed message board text*, which will help clarify what this property does if the user is confused. Finally, set the Default Value property to whatever you want the message board to say by default. Click the Apply Changes button and your property will now show up in the Widget Settings section. Try typing in a new value for your custom setting. Notice the widget will refresh and whatever you typed in will display in the message board. Now click the Save Widget button near the top-right of the page to continue.

You should now be on a page like the one shown in Figure 5-4, which allows you to manage and monitor your widgets. The Actions section of this page is a list of things you can do with your widgets and the Widget Effectiveness is a reminder of what's already been done and what's left to do. The Analytics section tells you how many people have viewed your widget (hits) and how many people have installed your widget (subscriptions).

Figure 5-4. Your widget dashboard page. Each widget you submit automatically gets its own dashboard page. This is where you can keep track of how your widget is doing and take the actions necessary to make it do better.

Testing Your Widget

The last step before you publish your widget is to test it and make sure it works in each way it can be installed. To do this, click the Test Widget button on your widget dashboard page. This will take you to a page with three previews of your widget. Users can install widgets using a JavaScript, Flash, or MySpace Flash code snippet. In some cases, widgets will work in one but not the others. For example, if you had done the mouse-over and mouse-out states off of `stage` instead of your `cover` movie clip, your widget would not work with the Flash or MySpace Flash code snippet but would work with the JavaScript one. Not calling `stage` is the main thing you have to remember when developing widgets for WidgetBox. The other most common issue is links within your widget not working. MySpace disables all links in Flash widgets, but there are instructions on how to get around this at WidgetBox.com. For more information on this and other issues that can occur, go to
`http://docs.widgetbox.com/developers/guide/flash/#basics`.
Once you've verified your widget works properly in all three install types, check the "Yes, my widget looks good" checkbox and click the Edit Widget button near the top-right of the screen.

Publishing Your Widget

Now that you've completed all the prerequisites, you are ready to get it out in the open and on as many outlets as you can. Making your widgets available to the public is an easy task with WidgetBox. The first step is to get it in the WidgetBox gallery. Then you'll get it on all web sites that WidgetBox supports.

Submitting to the WidgetBox Gallery

You should now be back on the page where you can edit the settings of your widget and submit it to the WidgetBox gallery (if not, return to your widget dashboard and click the Edit Widget button). Now click the Submit to Gallery button and you'll end up on the page where you fill out all the necessary info to submit your widget. The Widget Name and Widget URL should already be filled out. The Top Tags are basically the categories that best describe your widget. I chose *Fun* and *Music* but other combinations could also be accurate. In the Tags field, enter words that describe your widget and separate each with a comma. For your widget, "robot, dance, music" would be an accurate list. Add as many as you can think of because these keywords help users find your widget. In the Description field below, explain what your widget is all about while keeping it short and sweet. The last field is a thumbnail for your widget. This is very important. You want something that will make the potential users get the general idea of your widget, while still wanting to find out more. Take an interesting screen shot of your robot, crop, and upload it. Now review the Content Guideline and check the checkbox at the top of the page which states that your widget is not violating this agreement (which basically says that you aren't using any copyrighted content). Finally, click the Submit to Gallery button at the top-right of the page. Your widget will not automatically be added to the gallery because each one must be approved by WidgetBox. You should receive an email within a day or two, indicating that it has been approved or disapproved.

Turning Your Widget into a Facebook and Bebo App

Setting up your widgets on Facebook and Bebo can be very confusing, but WidgetBox walks you through step-by-step and makes it simple. There is no need to lead you through the instructions so just click the Make a Facebook App and Make a Bebo App buttons on your widget dashboard page and follow the steps. The only prerequisite is that you must be a member of both of these sites if you are not already. Once you have gotten through the initial steps, you should end up on a page like the one shown in Figure 5-5, which is an overview of your Facebook or Bebo App. On the right-hand side of this page, there is a list of Next Steps that are important to complete in order to have your App displayed in the way you wish and be submitted to the Bebo or Facebook App Directory.

Note Although it can be difficult, there is a lot of value in learning how to turn your widget into a Facebook App without Widgetbox. You can do more with the Facebook API, user profile information, and news feeds which can definitely help with your app's success. There is also more revenue potential because you don't have to split it with Widgetbox. Check out *Facebook API Developer's Guide* by Wayne Graham if you're interested.

Figure 5-5. Once you've created your Facebook or Bebo App, you'll end up on a page like this one. From here you can add a Help Page for your users and get started on the next steps to complete your App.

Getting in Additional Galleries

WidgetBox also helps you get your widgets into MySpace, Orkut, Hi5, and iGoogle galleries. Click the Add to More Galleries button on the widget management page to start. Each one is straightforward, so I will not walk you through it. After you have completed this, you'll be done with the publishing and distribution of your widget and are ready to focus on promotion.

Promoting Your Widget

It is good that you've got your widget into many galleries, but it is not enough. You need to bring attention to your widget and let people know it exists. The simplest and free way is for you and people you know to add the widget to your personal web sites, social profiles, and blogs. To get it yourself, click on your widget and the Get Widget button on the widget preview page. A good way to get the people you know to add it, other than by word of mouth, is to use the widgets provided by WidgetBox. There are two types, one that the user clicks which takes them to WidgetBox to get your widget, and another that allows users to get your widget from wherever you embed it. These both can be found through your widget management page. Go to the first by clicking the Promote Your Widget button and the second by clicking the Distribute Your Widget button. Another way to promote your widget, one that will not be free but will most likely be very effective, is starting a WidgetBox campaign. This will get your widget featured across WidgetBox.com and other galleries. It may not be cheap but the good part is you only pay when your widget is installed. Unfortunately, there is not much online information on this but you can find out more by contacting WidgetBox. To do this, go to `http://www.widgetbox.com/info/advertisers/campaigns` and click the Contact us to get started button.

Capitalizing on Your Widget

Making money on your widgets is not easy but it is definitely possible. The most important thing to remember is to focus on creating a quality widget and properly promoting it. Once you've done that, if it becomes popular the opportunity for revenue will arrive. The easiest way to make money initially is to participate in WidgetBox's Dev Share program. This is available for your Facebook Apps and gets you fifty percent of any money that comes in from the advertisements being clicked that are displayed around your widget. To participate in this program, click the My Widgetbox tab and then click the Facebook icon next to your widget. On the following page, fill in your PayPal email (if you don't have one already, go get one at `http://www.paypal.com`—it's free) and check the box that states "Yeah, cut me in on the deal" in the Make Money? section. Another way to capitalize on your widget is targeted in-widget advertising. If your widget goes viral, WidgetBox can help you sell advertising space, which is probably the biggest revenue generating step you can take. Remember, don't focus on making money on your widget initially, focus on it going viral and the money will follow.

Summary

In this final chapter, you learned all the steps necessary to launch your widget onto the internet. Once there, you found out how to get your widget into the many different galleries out there. Last, you read about the various ways to promote and capitalize on widgets. Overall, making widgets is both fun and rewarding; so explore your creativity and use what you learned in this book to develop innovative, high-quality Flash widgets. Your first few may not be the ones to go viral, but keep plugging away, make sure you do all the steps for publishing and promotion, and you may just have the next number one widget in your hands.

Copyright

Creating Flash Widgets with Flash CS4 and ActionScript 3

© 2008 by John Arana

ISBN-13 (electronic): 978-1-4302-1585-1

ISBN-13 (paperback): 978-1-4302-1584-4

Distributed to the book trade in the United States by Springer-Verlag New York, Inc., 233 Spring Street, 6th Floor, New York, NY 10013, and outside the United States by Springer-Verlag GmbH & Co. KG, Tiergartenstr. 17, 69112 Heidelberg, Germany.

In the United States: phone 1-800-SPRINGER, fax 201-348-4505, e-mail orders@springer-ny.com, or visit http://www.springer-ny.com. Outside the United States: fax +49 6221 345229, e-mail orders@springer.de, or visit http://www.springer.de.

For information on translations, please contact Apress directly at 2855 Telegraph Ave, Suite 600, Berkeley, CA 94705. Phone 510-549-5930, fax 510-549-5939, e-mail info@apress.com, or visit http://www.apress.com.

Breinigsville, PA USA
07 March 2011
257024BV00009B/8/P